Peoplization
An Introduction to Social Life

Melvyn L. Fein
Kennesaw State University

KENDALL/HUNT PUBLISHING COMPANY
4050 Westmark Drive   Dubuque, Iowa 52002

Contents

A Social Animal: Living Together

LIFE IS WITH PEOPLE

Many years ago a large proportion of Eastern European Jews lived in small towns called *shtetles.* Deeply impoverished and separated from their Slavic neighbors by religion and culture, residents were profoundly dependent upon one another. The resultant emotional bonds, as depicted in *Fiddler on the Roof* and an ethnography called *Life Is with People,* sensitized them to each other's demands and made it plain that they could not live without each other. Although these attachments could sometimes be suffocating, as when young people were forced to marry partners selected by their parents, they helped define their identities and provided them with a secure place in the universe. Everyone knew that they were not only individuals, but also members of a tightly knit community.

In truth, we are all members of social communities. Some may be tighter than others, but all oblige us to live with people and for people. Like it or not, we human beings are social animals. We evolved to subsist together in groups that shape our goals and provide our most important motives. Who we are, and what we become, is not up to us alone. The very thoughts we have about ourselves, the things we eat, the shelters in which we reside, and the jobs we perform all have interpersonal antecedents. We human beings, to be human, must therefore first become peoplized. We must learn to fit into the communities of which we are a part. Only when we do can we achieve our individual potentials.

Sociologist Gary Alan Fine drives this point home by asking two compelling questions: What would you die for? What would you kill for? When students are posed these questions the answers are revealing. Mothers almost always begin by affirming that they would be willing to die for their children, whereas those without children assert a desire to protect their parents, and to a lesser extent their siblings. Other relatives and close friends likewise elicit expressions of support, but usually only after some prompting. Some students, generally men, proclaim a readiness to sacrifice their lives for their country, while others, normally women, express a willingness to die for their religion. Men, it should be noted, frequently affirm a desire to defend their wives, whereas women rarely reciprocate this sentiment. Their focus is on their young.

Missing from this inventory are assertions reflecting personal desire. No one proclaims a longing to perish for everlasting fame or to expire for a fortune as large as that of Croesus. This inclination remains even after the spotlight shifts to the second question. Here, students again express a willingness to kill for relatives, their country, and their faith. They explain that while homicide is distasteful, these are virtuous causes. Few, however, say that they would kill for money. Even when assured that they would not be caught, that the victim deserves to die, and that the reward would be in the hundreds of thousands of dollars, the minority bold enough to declare a readiness to act as executioner brings forth snickers from classmates. The closest most of these others come to a personal reason for killing is self-defense.

The point of this exercise is that the grounds given for both dying and killing are almost entirely social. Although we live in a country that celebrates individualism, it is the impact on others that most determines what people declare themselves prepared to do. In fact, we truly are social animals. Despite our egoism, we are inevitably oriented toward others. Even hermits who go out and live in the wilderness generally do so in response to socially prescribed beliefs. So strong is this predisposition that it not only determines what people say they will do, but what they actually do. As Fredrick II, the Holy Roman Emperor at the time of the Crusades, discovered approximately eight hundred years ago, we human beings do, in truth, perish for the sake of others.

A German by birth, Fredrick moved his court to Sicily after conquering southern Italy. Lured by a better climate and a more prosperous environment to this center of ethnic diversity, his new situation prompted fresh thoughts. Now living amidst Sicilians, he was exposed to a broad array of languages. Besides German and Italian, many of his subjects spoke Greek, while his clergy communicated in Latin, and the Moslems just across the Mediterranean conversed in Arabic. As if this weren't enough, a journey to the Holy Land exposed him to Hebrew and Aramaic. What, then, he wondered, was the language of God? When God was by himself, which vocabulary did he use? Personally devout, this seemed to Fredrick an absorbing conundrum.

In order to find out, the emperor devised an ingenious experiment. He took perhaps a half dozen infants away from their mothers and assigned them to be raised by skilled nurses. These nurses were instructed to take good care of their charges, but not to speak to them at all. The youngsters were to be well fed and well clothed, but otherwise left in ignorance of any particular language. Fredrick's hope was that when these babies did begin to speak, whatever language they articulated must be the language of God. Since their idiom would be uninfluenced by human contrivance, it would be a natural one that was fundamental to the design of the universe.

But Fredrick was to be disappointed. The children never did speak the language of God. Indeed, they never spoke at all—they all died. It seems that infants require more than good physical care in order to prosper. They also need human interaction. Merely feeding and clothing them cannot substitute for the warm comfort of bonding with a mother during their prelinguistic conversations. The giggling sound games and smiling eye contact that precede verbalizations give children a motive to live. Without these they lose their desire to remain alive.

Instead, they refuse to eat and they subsequently languish and die. This condition is termed *marasmus* or *failure to thrive*. Either way, it demonstrates just how essential human contact is for life itself.

If this example does not make the point—and it might not, for it is, after all, apocryphal—another may. Somewhat before Fredrick, St. Augustine, one of the doctors of the early Christian Church, preached to his flock that the men should not have sex with prostitutes. This may sound unremarkable, except for the rationale that he provided. The reason he gave was that these men could not be sure if their partner was their daughter, and incest was, of course, a sin. To the modern ear this sounds very peculiar. How could a man not know whether a woman was his daughter? How could he fail to recognize her when the two bedded down?

The answer to this puzzle was that in Augustine's day birth control was accomplished by exposing unwanted children to the elements. An unwelcome daughter might thus be placed on a hillside, by the side of the road, or at the door of the church. What occurred next was up to chance. Perhaps a fortunate wolf happened by to help himself to an easy dinner. Or maybe a childless couple stumbled over the infant and initiated an informal adoption. If later this little girl grew up to be a prostitute, her biological father might indeed have sex with her without recognizing their relationship. Nowadays this sounds farfetched, but in St. Augustine's day infantile exposure was so common that his audience readily made the connection.

It was not until relatively recent times that the exposure method of birth control came to seem barbaric. As Northern Europe entered the period that in retrospect has been labeled the Enlightenment, nations such as England and France became prosperous enough to institute a different solution. Instead of trusting to the vicissitudes of exposure, they established "foundling" hospitals. These precursors of orphanages were places to which abandoned infants could be taken and provided with the shelter and nourishment they needed in order to survive. The problem was that these babies received no more loving contact than did Fredrick's test subjects. They too died in large numbers, victims of marasmus. Four out of five apparently succumbed to the emotional isolation of their circumstances.

The moral of these instances is clear. People need other people if they are to thrive. But there is more to the story. Vulnerable individuals not only require social interaction to survive, many persons will literally kill themselves for social reasons. Most of us are aware of the Japanese custom of suicide. We know that when a person loses face, that is, when he (or she) brings dishonor to those close to him, death may be considered preferable to living with the shame. In recent years this practice has included high school students whose grades were not sufficient to gain entry to a prestigious university; in times past such individuals were likely to be samurai who dishonored their masters.

Fewer of us are aware of the traditional Japanese method of committing suicide. We have heard of *seppuku* and *hara-kiri,* but we don't know exactly what these practices entail. *Seppuku* means ritual suicide, whereas *hara-kiri* denotes belly cutting. A samurai who was obliged to perform the latter followed an elaborate ceremony that culminated in thrusting a short sword into his stomach. He then drew this weapon across his abdomen and, if he had any strength left, pulled it upward toward his heart. At this he expired, or, if he did not, he had his head lopped off by an assistant.

Obviously hara-kiri is not an exercise in which one chooses to engage just for the fun of it. One does not suddenly arise one morning with an irresistible desire to eviscerate oneself. To the contrary, a person does so because he is socially expected to do so. Because others believe it is the proper thing to do, the dishonored person also agrees that it is the appropriate course. Despite the unbearable pain of such a death, the individual is motivated to end his life in this socially prescribed manner.

A similar kind of extreme social motivation was revealed in the fiery deaths of World War II kamikaze pilots. They tied good luck bands around their foreheads and strapped themselves into doomed planes before immolating themselves for the glory of the emperor. Middle Eastern suicide bombers are a comparable modern counterpart. Convinced that if they martyr themselves for their religion they will gain immediate entry into heaven, they blow themselves to bits to further a violent social movement. They even film the event to testify to their delight in joining Allah.

The significance of all this is that if we are going to understand ourselves, we must understand our social selves. We not only have to understand how our bodies work, or how our brains operate, but also how we become peoplized. Why are we social in the first place, and in what ways are we social? In particular, what are the consequences of needing to be with people? How does our affinity for living with other human beings influence the choices we make or determine the pleasures we obtain? More than this, what can go wrong from being social—and just as important, what can go right? Are there pitfalls and opportunities more recognizable to those who are self-aware?

LIFE IS WITH LOTS OF PEOPLE

How many close friends do you have? Do they number in the dozens or the hundreds? Former president Bill Clinton claimed to have many thousands of intimate friends. Most of us are not that lucky. When asked with how many others we would feel comfortable sharing personal secrets or borrowing large sums of money, the usual answer is something like five. Telephone companies have come to the same conclusion and thus offer calling circles of this size. Larger numbers apparently make us uncomfortable. We do not mind having numerous acquaintances, but intimates are another matter. For intimate relationships we desire people we can trust, and trust is something that takes time and effort to develop.

This preference is seemingly built into the sort of social creatures we are. It appears to be part of our evolutionary heritage. Once upon a time, we human beings lived in small hunter-gatherer communities. As recently as twelve thousand years ago all of our ancestors resided in such groups. Sociologists refer to these as *Gemeinschaft* societies. In their original form they consisted of small bands of between 100 and 150 persons. This included everyone—men, women, and children, from the oldest to the youngest. Mostly related to one another, their interactions were typically face to face and very personal. It is here that evolution instilled a preference for being intimate with only a comparative few.

Nevertheless, today we do not live within such communities. Ours is a much larger world. We inhabit what sociologists refer to as a *Gesellschaft* society. Ours is a mass, market society. It is a civilization filled with millions of others, the vast majority of whom are strangers to one another. Individuals who have never met, and probably never will meet, are nonetheless dependent upon one another for their survival. They may see each other on the street, or glance at one another while driving down the highway, but never share a word, or have any desire to do so. But still they could not live as they do without each other.

Economist Milton Friedman made this clear through a simple exercise. He would hold up a pen or pencil and ask his classes how many people it took to make this writing implement. The typical answer was a few dozen, but, as Friedman explained, the real answer was many tens of thousands. With a pen, one must not begin with the persons operating the machines that turned out this item, but with the metal of which its shell was constructed. Aluminum, for instance, begins with bauxite, which is mined in such places as Jamaica. What, then, of the men who did the mining? And what of the machines with which they performed this extraction? What also of the metal of which these machines were made or the men who extracted the ore that went into making these? The numbers involved in fashioning the pen plainly begin to grow exponentially, but no mention has yet been made of the trucks that bring the bauxite to where it is processed or the ships that transport the metal to where it is fabricated into pens or of those who construct these ships, and so on.

Gesellschaft societies are shot through with intersecting networks of mutual dependency. Not only pens and pencils, but virtually all of the products upon which our lives depend are produced by people we do not know. Literally millions of others go into providing us with the food, shelter, and clothing upon which our survival hinges. Our hunter-gatherer ancestors went out and picked the berries that they later ate, but who today grows most of their own vegetables? More pointedly, who raises the chickens that eventually become part of a chicken parmesan dinner? Most people nowadays do not even pluck their own chickens, let alone nurture them to maturity. What also of our houses? How many of us hammer the two-by-fours that comprise their frame or install the kitchen cabinets in which we will house our favorite dishes? Or what about our clothes? How many of us even know how to weave cloth? All of this makes us reliant on the good graces of a myriad of strangers.

If the truth be told, we are also dependent upon these others for our personal safety. In a world crammed with strangers, we must trust to their good intentions on a daily basis. Consider how vulnerable we are when driving down a highway. It is absolutely essential that the other drivers by whom we are surrounded stay in their lanes. If they suddenly decided to swerve into us, there would be little we could do. Nor could we protect ourselves if drug manufactures switched from packaging aspirin to marketing poison or if doctors decided to stop washing their hands before they operated on us. We expect these strangers to behave in predicable ways, which by and large they do. They may not know us, but we go about our usual rounds assured that they will not violate our trust in them.

So familiar is this *Gesellschaft* environment that we take it for granted. Although our ancestors evolved to occupy a very different sort of life space, we have grown accustomed to conducting our lives in environments filled with lots of people. Despite the fact that we are more comfortable with those we know well, we reside with equanimity alongside people we do not know and whose intentions we may not fathom. The question is thus: How is this possible? How do we remain relaxed and confident in what should be a stressful atmosphere? Does peoplization have anything to do with this? In other words, must we learn to dwell with numerous other people?

One of the great unappreciated mysteries of human existence is how our species transformed from living in *Gemeinschaft* societies to dwelling in *Gesellschaft* environments. Our nearest relatives, that is, chimpanzees, never made this transition. Nor has any other large species. What has enabled us, and only us, to subsist in immense cities or to construct nation-states? What has permitted us to depend on strangers a half a world away when no other significant mammal does so? We, to be sure, construct little pockets of *Gemeinschaft* amidst all this *Gesellschaft;* we rely on small circles of friends and relatives in this world full of strangers. But is this enough? Does this alone allow us to cooperate with outsiders? And if not, what else is needed? What accounts for our being able to live and work among so many others we do not know?

LIFE IS AGAINST PEOPLE—OR NOT

Let us consider two fundamental premises and the consequences of putting them together. For the moment, let us suspend our most critical faculties and see if we can accept this pair of theses. The first is that we human beings are, for the most part, selfish creatures. Each of us usually places our own interests above those of others. We generally want what we want and are not troubled if we get more than others do. For each of us, we are, as they say, number one. Our comfort and our welfare are reckoned to be more important than the comfort or welfare of outsiders. Indeed, we may not even notice their distress when compared with our own. For most of us, this assertion seems obvious. It describes the bedrock of human existence.

The second premise may be less evident. It is that we human beings are the most successful killers that have ever inhabited this planet. Each and every one of us has the ability, if not the propensity, to slaughter any other one of us, almost whenever we want. This may seem absurd in that we lack the physiological killing tools of most other carnivores. We do not, for instance, possess the sharp teeth or claws of lions, the talons of birds of prey, or the speed of cheetahs and great white sharks. Confronted by almost any one of these creatures, we would be at a marked disadvantage. We would become the prey, and they the predator.

But we do not kill with teeth or fingernails. We do so with tools. We slay with knives and guns that are controlled by supple brains. So proficient have we been at devising implements with which to deprive other creatures of life that we can execute animals are large as whales and as small as microbes—and anything in between. We are surely able to do so to one another. We are even able do so with persons who are larger and stronger than we are. All it takes is an appropriately conceived strategy. A little poison surreptitiously introduced into another's soup or a pillow held down over an offending bed partner's face may do the trick. One can even run an enemy over with an automobile, and if this does not succeed, one can put the vehicle into reverse and try again. The potentially lethal plans are endless.

In putting these two premises together we come up with an intriguing mystery. If we are all selfish and if we are all great killers, why do we not murder those who get in our way for the sake of an immediate advantage? If another person has a house we covet, why not execute him and move in ourselves? Or if several people in our class are getting better grades than we are, why not assassinate them so as to move up to the top of the curve? It would all be so simple. Get them out of the way and get what we want. When confronted with this prospect, however, many people respond that this would not be moral; that it would not be the right thing to do. But why should that stop us? Just because others admonish us that this sort of conduct is improper, why not go ahead and silence them too? What is the thin, reedy voice of morality compared with our ability to exterminate those who interfere with our desires?

This is not a newly minted problem. It occurred to Thomas Hobbes almost four hundred years ago. The way he framed it was this: If in a state of nature, that is, if in an environment in which each person can behave just as he pleases, one person craves what another has, what is to stop the first from killing the second and appropriating whatever he wants? The answer, according to Hobbes, was: nothing. Under such conditions, everyone would be everyone else's enemy and there would exist what Hobbes termed "a war of all against all." In this atmosphere, one where selfishness ran rampant, no one would ever be safe. No one could ensure that someone else tomorrow would not steal what he stole today. Again in the words of Hobbes, under these circumstances life would be "nasty, brutish, and short." Theft would be normal, but so would insecurity and murder.

What was necessary, according to Hobbes, was someone to protect us from ourselves. He assumed that people would eventually realize that it was not in their interest to endure unrestrained selfishness and that they would get together to draw up a compact in which they agreed to submit to the authority of one of their strongest members. This person, whom Hobbes refers to as the Leviathan, would gain further strength by having his own powers backed up by those of his subjects. In other words, Hobbes believed that people required a sovereign (in his day, a king) to control their selfishness. Not a voluntary morality, but a potent government, would preserve their safety from their inherent greed. Only this would allow people to live together in relative harmony.

Of course, not everyone has agreed with this prescription. Many have been uneasy with the potential despotism of such an autocrat. They have not understood why anyone would want to submerge himself or herself to an absolute ruler. Some have believed this to be unnecessary one such was Jean-Jacques Rousseau. Residing in France about a century after Hobbes, he was aware of the idea of a social compact, but was convinced his predecessor had got it wrong. Rousseau asserted that people were not born selfish, but rather were innately loving. Left to their own devices, each would help others. Their normal impulses were analogous to those of uncorrupted children. Like toddlers who are spontaneously solicitous of the welfare of their mothers, they would instinctively seek to comfort and support one another.

For Rousseau, the villain of the piece was government. Turning Hobbes on his head, he wrote that it is government that ruins fundamentally unselfish individuals by handing out honors to some, but not to others. In Rousseau's state of nature, human beings were noble savages. They were in touch with their inner feelings and sensitive to their external surroundings. They were, in short, like the American Indians depicted in Disney's version of the Pocahontas story. Totally in harmony with their fellows and always prepared to share their common bounty with those in need, they experienced no desire for interpersonal friction. None sought to puff themselves up or rule over the others; hence none did.

What destroyed this harmony was the invention of property. Only after one person fenced in a piece of land and called it his own would there be conflicts over ownership. Only after this fateful development could one person accumulate more than another. Before this, selfishness was impossible because there was nothing over which to be selfish. It was, therefore, government—through protecting property rights and distributing them unequally—that caused the problem. All would be well if these authorities were limited. All would be solved if social leaders were responsive to the "general will" instead of to the impulses of a particular sovereign. Not surprisingly, Rousseau hoped for a revolution that would enable people to return to their loving roots.

Who, then, is correct? Are we fundamentally selfish killers who must be protected from ourselves by a powerful government, or are we selfless innocents who must be defended against a government that is intent on corrupting us? Opinions are divided. Generally speaking, contemporary conservatives believe that we are selfish and prone to evil, whereas liberals are convinced that we are essentially loving and, were we freed of elite exploitation, would reside in collective harmony. Depending on which of these views is correct, the implications for peoplization are profound. On the one hand, we would require externally enforced rules to enable us to live together; on the other, cooperative behaviors would emerge instinctively from our very nature.

In fact, we seem to be a little bit of both. People are selfish and dangerous. But they are also loving. People do require external rules, but they also possess generous impulses. We are not simply one or the other, but an unpredictable blend of the two. What enables us to live together in large social groups is therefore more complicated than submitting to an all-powerful ruler or trusting to utopian cooperation. The cement that enables large societies to remain intact has many dimensions, dimensions that we will shortly explore.

In the meantime, it is interesting to note that Rousseau himself did not live the sort of life his theories might suppose him to have led. He was far from an uncomplicated man who cast his goodwill in every direction. Having arrived in prerevolutionary Paris after a circuitous journey that began in Geneva, Switzerland, he was determined to make his mark. Upon winning a prestigious essay contest, he hoped to be acclaimed in the intellectual salons presided over by aristocratic women. But to do this, he needed to dress the part. Rousseau also coveted the romantic attentions of his hostesses, yet he understood that, as a commoner, they would not favor him sexually.

Rousseau's solution was to take up with a working-class girl whom he kept in a back street of Paris and visited as his appetites required. Together they sired five children. But as each one appeared, Rousseau was presented with a dilemma. If he supported them, he would not have the funds needed to purchase the clothing necessary to appear in stylish salons. He instead decided to send each in turn to the foundling hospital. Yet, as we have learned, this probably condemned four out of five to death—hardly consistent with the qualities of a loving parent. What, then, are we to make of Rousseau's theories? Was his belief that we are inherently loving contradicted by his personal behaviors? Or was his conduct evidence that even he had been corrupted by the inequalities of modern civilization? Each of us must decide for ourselves.

SEEKING ANSWERS

If we are social creatures, what sort of social creatures are we? And how are we to find out? We could simply depend upon our intuitions, but our intuitions are frequently inconsistent. What seems to be true to some people is not always evident to others. The way out of this difficulty is through disciplined observations. If we are careful and systematic in the manner in which we scrutinize the human condition, and if we draw from the evidence so collected only that which logically follows from it, we may arrive at trustworthy conclusions. Such is the aim of science. Science should not be a mystery. It is merely an orderly means of seeking to acquire knowledge; in this case knowledge about peoplization.

One of the primary social sciences is sociology. Sociology is about the study of groups of people. Sociology deals with social behavior at every level. It covers everything from dyads to world systems—everything from small family groups to huge nation-states. Sociologists observe how people interact, but in addition, they attempt to figure out why they do so in one way rather than another. The idea is to try to predict how people will behave in particular circumstances. As a result, sociologists derive hypotheses from their observations and then test these in subsequent events. If their conjectures prove correct, they seek to build on these; if they do not, they revise them in the hope of getting closer to the truth.

Another of the principal social sciences is psychology. Psychology is about the study of individual psyches, that is, about how the human mind works. For most people psychology is more familiar than is sociology. In an individualistic society such as our own, it is the science that is usually thought best able to help understand other people. But a perplexing question arises. In what way does psychology differ from sociology? Is there a hard and fast line that divides the study of individuals from that of groups? Specifically, does psychology never investigate the relationships between individuals, or does sociology habitually eschew examining the inclinations of single persons?

In fact, psychology regularly explores interpersonal territory. In studying personal motives, for instance, it asks about the relationships between individuals and their parents, especially when the former were young. There is even a subdomain of psychology called community psychology. Sociology, for its part, would not get far in explaining complex social interactions if it did not also inquire into the motivations of the separate participants. What they independently want and believe is integral to determining how they respond to one another. Groups are, in short, composed of individuals and thus cannot be appreciated without studying single members as well.

So what is the difference between sociology and psychology? To ask this question in another way: Is social psychology a part of sociology or of psychology? The answer is that it is integral to both and that there is thus an inevitable overlap between these two social sciences. Each may believe that the other poaches on its rightful territory, but neither would be complete without learning from its rival. Perhaps the best way to distinguish them is to refer to their starting points. Sociology begins with groups and works inward toward individuals, whereas psychology starts with individuals and works outward to groups. As such, they differ more in their perspective than in their subject matter.

This brings us to another core social science, namely anthropology. It too studies human behavior, but in still another context. Anthropologists have historically studied communities that are either long ago or far away. Many are archeologists who dig for evidence of civilizations that have disappeared into the mists of time, while others are cultural specialists who travel to remote corners of the globe to investigate preliterate societies. Sociologists, in contrast, have been more concerned with contemporary Western civilizations. They look to the here and now rather than the far away.

And yet, as with psychology and sociology, there is an overlap. Anthropologists have not been content to deal only with remote communities. They have in recent years applied their techniques to studying contemporary medical systems and inner-city cultures. This might be considered scientific imperialism, but if it is, it has been reciprocated by sociologists such as Max Weber who have researched ancient China and India in order to throw light on modern civilizations. Here too, however, the best way to understand what is happening is to interpret it as a difference in perspective. Once again, one discipline begins in one place and the other in another—the one from far away and long ago, the other from the here and now, and then they meet in the middle.

Finally, there are the socially oriented disciplines of economics and political science. They too deal with interpersonal interactions, but from a much more circumscribed standpoint. Economics specializes in how people earn a living and political science is concerned with how they govern themselves. Obviously, these both involve group dynamics and might therefore be considered part of the sociological mandate, but they each have independent historical roots and specialized technical means of studying their subject matter. Just as important, both have illuminated the nature of human communities in ways that sociology has not.

The bottom line is that if we are to understand how human beings become peoplized, we must draw from all of these social sciences. Each contributes information that the others do not. Just as significant, each contributes details that illuminate the facts that have been unearthed by the others. A jealous parochialism is therefore unhelpful to the overall objective of answering our questions about how and why people live together, especially in large groups. In this present volume the focus will be on sociological contributions, but these are neither exhaustive nor exclusive. They are, however, useful, and arguably essential. So let us proceed, and see what we can learn.

Questions

1. What would you die, or kill, for?
2. How many close friends do you have?
3. Are human beings primarily killers or lovers?
4. Why did Rousseau behave as he did?

Selected Readings

Hobbes, T. 1956. *Leviathan; Part I.* Chicago: Henry Regnery Co.

Rousseau, J. J. [1762] 1968. *The Social Contract* (translated by Maurice Cranston). New York: Penguin Books.

Toennies, F. [1887] 1966. *Community and Society.* New York: Harper Row.

Zborowski, M., and Herzog, E. 1962. *Life Is with People.* New York: Schocken Press.

2

The Sociological Perspective: Taking a Social Point of View

A PECULIAR SCIENCE

Have you ever been on an elevator? Of course you have. Almost everyone who lives in a modern *Gesellschaft* society has been at one time or another. Then it should be easy to answer the following questions. How do people behave when they use an elevator? Are there any peculiar ways that they act? If so, what are these? But beyond this, why do they act in such a manner? Are there reasons that they conduct themselves in this fashion within this environment, but not in others? In others words, can you describe, and then analyze, elevator behavior?

Some things surely come to mind. One is that people in elevators face toward the front of the cubicle. They situate themselves so that they are looking toward the doors and not the back wall. Perhaps less obvious will be the pattern in which they position themselves. When one person enters, he or she typically gravitates toward the center of the back wall. If a second person comes on board, the first generally moves toward a back corner, while the newcomer fills the other corner. Should a third or forth enter their space, these others will likely occupy the front corners. All then patiently scrutinize the fascinating little numerals above the front door. Rarely will they speak to each other or give each other more than a polite smile.

When these behaviors are described to people, they almost invariably nod in agreement. Having been there many times, they concede that this is usually what takes place. They may not initially have been able to articulate this pattern, but they recognize it once someone else puts it into words. If further asked why people behave in these ways, they once again may be stymied. They know what happens, but a mental block prevents them from enunciating what they inchoately sense.

If under these circumstances they are told that the reason for this elevator behavior concerns a need for personal space, they concur. They agree that people carry around a kind of bubble of privacy. Most of us feel uncomfortable if others intrude into the two- to three-foot area of separation we demand. This desire for space becomes all the more acute when confined to small quarters with several strangers. Each of us then attempts to pretend that we are alone. The weak smiles so frequent under the circumstances are merely a device for engaging in civil inattention. One does not want to insult others, but neither does one want to invite them into one's space.

All this makes sense once it is explained, but we might not perceive it if it were not first so explained. This turns out to be a regular feature of our social world. We usually understand enough about what is going on to behave in the expected manner, but we may not be conscious of how we achieve this. Indeed, we often come up with explanations that do not fit the facts. Take the case of the "Latin lover." Many Northern Europeans believe that Southern European men are particularly aggressive lovers. They appear to come on faster than is appropriate. But things are not what they seem.

The reason for this disjunction has to do with personal space. Northern Europeans tend to require a larger bubble than do Southern Europeans. This means that if a man from Italy approaches a woman from Scandinavia, he may attempt to get closer to her than she finds comfortable. When she then backs away, he steps closer in order to reestablish the distance he finds congenial. What subsequently follows is a sort of dance in which she continues to retreat until backed into a corner. From her perspective, he is moving too fast, and hence is being sexually aggressive, whereas from his, he is simply being polite.

Our social worlds are intimately familiar to us, but this does not mean that they are sufficiently well understood to be correctly interpreted. One of the implications of this is that people often dismiss sociology as common sense. They are confident that they understand its subject matter without having to have it explicated by specialists. Most are convinced that they are sufficiently expert on their own to get by without the pompous theorizing of self-important social scientists.

In this belief, ordinary persons have a point. They do understand much of their social world without assistance. If they did not, they would make egregious mistakes that might make it impossible to survive. Having spent years living within a social world, they acquire numerous hard lessons and many penetrating insights. To treat them as if they were completely naïve about social matters would be both wrong and insulting. Nevertheless, people are like the proverbial fish who live within water so constantly that they do not perceive the medium. People also take for granted, and hence do not consciously perceive, that in which they are continuously immersed.

Sociology is therefore a peculiar science. It regularly deals with the familiar, while attempting to articulate it in such a manner that it becomes consciously recognizable. In this, the discipline endeavors to describe accurately that which is there to be seen, but also to clarify the causal connections in what is apprehended. It is these explanations that are the most difficult to get correct, but that, when they are appropriately portrayed, can be particularly rewarding. When this occurs, these accounts make it possible to achieve our goals more effectively. When people accurately perceive what is happening, and why, they can better plan how to attain what they desire, including effective peoplization.

One of the chief obstacles to this objective is bias. Precisely because we human beings are social animals, we care about our social world—indeed, we care very much. Because we want things to happen as we desire, we frequently misperceive them. Wishful thinking replaces careful observation and we are offended by characterizations of the facts that contradict our hopes. As bright as we may be, our prejudices overtake our good sense and we don't even listen to people with opinions inconsistent with our own.

This propensity complicates sociological research. Because sociologists too are human beings, many investigators cease pursuing the truth and become apologists for their favorite beliefs. This is the case for both sides of the political spectrum. Liberals and conservatives alike stubbornly defend their moral commitments at the expense of advancing knowledge. What can happen is illustrated by a study sponsored by the American Association of University Women (AAUW). It sought to demonstrate that girls are shortchanged by the American education system, but inadvertently became a case study in putting a heavy finger on the observational scales.

What the association's investigators breathlessly reported to a receptive media was that boys were at least seven times more likely than girls to be called upon by their elementary school teachers. Even though these teachers were women, they favored males by showering them with extra attention. This conveyed the message that the girls were less important than boys, which had a devastating impact on the girls' self-esteem. They consequently entered adolescence primed to be less successful than their male peers. The AAUW trumpeted this as incontestable evidence that girls needed a fairer deal from a prejudiced society.

All of this sounded both alarming and definitive. How could teachers be so unjust to girls? How could they be so lopsided? The trouble was, however, that the study itself was replete with bias. First, when the data was reexamined by less committed observers, they found that boys were called upon perhaps only three times as often as girls. But it was the reason for this disparity that was most revealing. The boys were called upon because they were being more disruptive in class. The teachers were asking them to answer questions as a result of their not paying attention and/or their making a commotion. How this negative interest was supposed to help the self-esteem of the boys was a mystery, except to the initial investigators.

Second, although the girls did less well than the boys on tests of self-esteem, this was not associated with academic failure. In fact, girls got better grades in high school than boys. They were also going to college in growing numbers, where once again they excelled. To claim that girls were somehow at a disadvantage because of the way they were treated by their grammar school teachers was simply not borne out by subsequent developments. These developments were nonetheless invisible to researchers who began their work determined to document gender-based injustices.

They had much in common with investigators on the other side of the question, who a century earlier had concluded that females would not do well in school because they were not as intelligent as males. Their evidence came from the comparative size of male and female brains. More specifically, they found that males had bigger brains, which therefore meant that they must be smarter. The problem with this reasoning was that brain size is not correlated with intelligence. But worse than this, the explanation of why the men have larger brains—which they do—is that they are physically larger. The disparity has nothing to do with relative intellect.

The significance of these examples is that we must all be wary of seeing what we want to see. The temptation to perceive only evidence favorable to our beliefs is universal. So is the inclination to interpret facts to suit our preferences. Sadly, there is no foolproof cure for these penchants. The best we can do is to be on guard against them. Thus, if we find ourselves looking at the same data as another person of goodwill, but coming to an opposite conclusion, something is wrong. One, or both, of us must be in error. In this case, we ought first to look to ourselves to determine if we are being victimized by our personal biases. After this we should look to the other person to determine whether he or she is being misled by corresponding biases. Even so, we may continue to be deceived, but at least we will have given ourselves an opportunity to get closer to the truth.

RESEARCH TECHNIQUES

Many people believe that social research is synonymous with experimentation. Psychologists, in particular, are fond of asserting that knowledge is acquired by carefully constructing experiments in which there is an experimental group and a control group, the two of which are distinguished by the ways in which their independent and dependent variables are arranged. If one group is exposed to an identified condition, but the other is not, it is possible to compare the consequences of this to determine if there is a causal connection between the variables. Years of research have demonstrated that this is a productive means of acquiring new information—it can indeed teach us how events are related.

Unfortunately, this method is not always available in sociology. Social psychologists and small-group researchers have been able to manipulate their subjects to come to significant conclusions, but much of the subject matter of sociology is not open to such manipulation. If, for instance, one wished to determine whether capitalism or socialism leads to greater freedom, one cannot assign one society to be capitalist and another to be socialist. Researchers simply do not possess this power. They must instead depend on natural experiments. They can compare the capitalist and socialist societies that currently exist or have existed. These assessments may not meet experimental protocols, but they are the best that can be mustered.

Nor would experimentation always be ethical. One cannot, for example, arbitrarily divide a college class into an experimental and control group and assign grades in terms of gender or ethnic affiliation. To do so would be grossly unfair and a breach of the participants' basic human rights. Nor could one capriciously remove children from their parents, or get people fired from their jobs, to see how they will react. The Nazis engaged in this sort of research in their concentration camps, but few of us would wish to repeat their excesses, no matter how much data this might produce.

Happily, we can use other methods. Sociology is primarily an observational science. It depends on disciplined surveillance of how groups of people behave. Some may believe that such observations are too inherently disorderly to be scientific, that their lack of controls makes it impossible to obtain reliable comparisons. What these commentators forget is that there are other observational sciences. Astronomy and geology, and even anthropology, have been able to make great strides without possessing the ability to manipulate their subjects. The crux of the matter is whether one can be careful, and relatively unbiased, in making one's observations.

One of the unique formats utilized by sociologists in gathering information has been participant observation. Researchers have joined the groups they wished to understand and sought to examine them from the inside. This presents hazards, especially in terms of bias, but also opportunities. There is some data to which only trusted participants are allowed access. In the early days of gender research, when homosexuality was socially scorned, only investigators who went underground and approached their subjects in their world were able to witness their lifestyles. The same has applied to gang research and to some organizational studies.

Nevertheless, sociologists more commonly utilize structured interviews. They ask people what they do in various circumstances and record the results. Those investigators who are able to elicit trust have been able to unearth significant findings through this method. One of the advantages of this technique is that it allows for follow-up questions. The researcher who is responsive to his or her subjects can probe to discover what might not initially be revealed. The problem with this approach is that it is time consuming and expensive. This usually limits the number of individuals that can be studied and therefore the applicability of the findings.

Greater breadth is often achieved by utilizing survey instruments. Large numbers of persons can be asked to complete questionnaires from which meaningful information is then statistically extracted. Here the difficulty is that the questions asked must be determined in advance and therefore must be restricted in scope. Nor can they be adjusted in midstream to take advantage of unexpected results. There is also the further difficulty in that a survey sample may not accurately reflect the population one wishes to understand. This was particularly problematic in the early days of utilizing questionnaires to study sexual behavior. Those who volunteered to fill out the surveys tended to be exhibitionists. In addition, people often lie about sensitive issues. They may claim to have had more (or less) partners than is accurate. Nevertheless, survey research has become increasingly sophisticated. Indeed, so customary has it become that nowadays it is almost synonymous with sociological research.

A great deal of research is likewise conducted by way of data analysis. The things that people do frequently leave residues behind that can then be examined for clues about what takes place in groups, and why. One might, in this case, comb through the client records in a psychiatric hospital in order to determine the incidence of mental illness among designated populations. Or one might engage in a content analysis of consumer magazines to figure out if transformations in clothing styles are related to modifications in gender roles. Perhaps most important of all are such sources as the U.S. Census. Shifts in demographic figures can be very revealing about trends in lifestyles, as in the evolution of suburbanization.

Much of this accumulation of information would be less instructive than it is without concurrent advances in statistical analysis. Tests for statistical significance have proven essential in determining which correlations are meaningful and which are not. Statistical manipulations can also tease out the variables that need to be investigated. Several items that initially seem to be distinct may on closer investigation be discovered to be part of a larger pattern. [See Addendum]

Finally, it must be understood that science is not always about finding what is true. Just as important—perhaps more important—it is about determining what is *not* true. If social scientists put forth a hypothesis, it is significant only if it is open to disconfirmation. If it is not, then it is a tautology. It may seem to tell us something, but if it is true no matter what, then it does not really tell us anything. Genuine knowledge is subject to modification and growth. Authentic science leads to surprises and not just to a restatement of that which one already believes.

THE LARGE PICTURE—MACRO THEORIES

Were science merely about accumulating disjointed facts it would not be very useful. Research that only provides isolated bits of information could not provide us with an overview of what is happening. We would possess lots of pieces of the puzzle, but would lack a coherent picture of the whole. In short, we would not know how the parts fit together. For this we are dependent upon theories. Theories entail articulated sets of hypotheses. They are large-scale explanations of events. Theories place facts in context. They tell us which pieces of information are important and why they are related or unrelated to each other.

In recent years, three theoretical frameworks have dominated sociology. Two of these are macro theories and one is a micro theory. The macro theories attempt to put society as a whole in context. They look at the big picture and attempt to explain how entire societies operate. Micro theories, in contrast, look to the small picture. They seek to explain how individual human beings interrelate. It is then hoped that these small exchanges will add up to a larger portrait. Macro and micro theories are thus different, but they can both contribute to an integrated view of the whole.

On the macro level there is currently an ongoing dispute between structural-functionalists and conflict theorists. Perhaps the best representative of the structural-functional school is Emile Durkheim. Working in France about a century ago, he sought to explain society by emphasizing what is referred to as an "organic analogy." He begins his account with a body—let us say a human body. He then notes that it is apparent that this body is composed of a number of differentiated parts. These parts are called organs and they fit together in a structured manner. Thus, the body has a heart, a liver, two lungs, a brain, and so forth. Only together do they constitute a complete organism.

But there is more. These discrete organs have distinct functions. The heart pumps blood, the liver produces digestive juices, the lungs introduce oxygen to the system, and the brain organizes complex behaviors. Each of these contributions is vital to the survival of the whole. Indeed, no separate organ could survive without efforts of the other major organs. All benefit from the tasks in which the others specialize. So vital are these specializations that none could stay alive, save for the work that the others perform.

Durkheim argues that societies are similarly organized. They too are divided into parts that are related to each other in an identifiable manner. Moreover, these parts specialize in identifiable functions. According to Durkheim, societies are characterized by a division of labor. Different players within these communities occupy different niches in which they perform dissimilar tasks. Some are farmers, others truck drivers, and still others soldiers or politicians. They then relate to each other in terms of their respective roles.

But these roles also have functions. The farmers produce the food that the others consume. The truck drivers bring this bounty to market where it is available to be consumed by laypersons. The soldiers protect the community from external threats and the politicians help to organize communal endeavors. What each does differs from what the others do, but all benefit from their respective contributions. As with the body, none could survive—or prosper—without the functional cooperation of the others. Societies, in short, are as functionally structured as are biological organisms.

Durkheim went a step farther and sought to explain how societies maintain their integrity through these means. Aware that human groups have progressed from small-scale *Gemeinschaft* arrangements to large-scale *Gesellschaft* ones, he asked what held them together under these varying circumstances. In his language, what provided their solidarity? The resultant theory was that they depend on different mechanisms according to their size. Small hunter-gatherer groups are said to rely on mechanical solidarity, whereas modern mass-market societies trust in organic solidarity.

Mechanical solidarity is alleged to derive from the sympathy that people who perform the same tasks are able to feel for one another. Thus, if everyone is a hunter, each can understand the demands made of the others and make adjustments so that they effectively cooperate. Organic solidarity, however, is different. In *Gesellschaft* societies, most people are strangers to one another. They would have difficulty feeling sympathy for persons they never actually meet. Mass-market societies instead count on the interdependence of their constituents. In this case, people cooperate with one another because they recognize that their individual survival is dependent upon the efforts of the others. They may not know many farmers, but they feel sympathy toward them because they realize that their own welfare hinges on the welfare of those who produce their food.

Durkheim's universe is thus a world in which consensus is critical. People remain loyal to their own societies because it is in their interest to do so. They care about their fellow human beings and cooperate with them because to do otherwise would bring disaster upon all. Conflict theorists, however, find this absurd. Their universe, in sharp contrast, is filled with strife. Their system depicts some people as taking advantage of others, and therefore as deserving of being resisted. Far from consensus, they perceive societies as fraught with discord.

The foremost critical theorist is none other than Karl Marx. There have been many variations on his conception since it was formulated in the middle of the nineteenth century, but its underlying principles remain influential to this day. For Marx, society was divided into competing social classes. Each of these groupings sought to dominate the whole by controlling the means of production. In the past, European aristocrats were able to achieve this by monopolizing land ownership, but in recent times it has been capitalists who have taken over. By obtaining exclusive ownership of the machines that produce the lion's share of contemporary goods and services, they are able to dictate how society operates. This alternation of ruling classes is referred to by Marx as a "material dialectic" and is said to determine the contours of history.

Opposed to the capitalists are the proletarians. They are the workers in the capitalist-controlled factories. Although it is their labors that create the value inherent in the goods they turn out, they do not own what they produce. This belongs to their bosses, who sell it to enhance their personal profit. Owners receive what Marx called surplus value, whereas their workers are allowed only enough to maintain their productive capacity. In time, the owners accumulate massive wealth by exploiting the efforts of their employees, while the workers struggle along on subsistence wages. For all intents and purposes wage slaves, they live in misery amidst a world of plenty.

Why, then, do the proletarians submit? It is because, says Marx, they are victims of false consciousness. Their bosses tell them that the way production is organized is in their interests too, which they believe because they perceive their bosses as authorities. Furthermore, they are also both coerced and manipulated into submission. For one thing, should they protest their low wages, they will be threatened with dismissal. An owner will point to the job applicants at the factory gate, the so-called reserve army of the unemployed, and suggest that they would be happy with the income that a disgruntled employee spurns. For another, workers are encouraged to believe in religion, which Marx characterizes as the opiate of the masses. If the proletarians can be convinced that they will receive the reward for their humility in heaven, they may be less inclined to challenge the dominance of the capitalists in this world.

To Marx, and conflict theorists in general, this is grossly unjust. They prefer more egalitarian arrangements. To this end, they seek to stimulate a revolution. Marx declared that proletarians should rise up and overthrow their bosses, that they had nothing to lose but their chains. Contemporary conflict theorists are less sanguinary. They prefer social movements that encourage social democracy. The final objective, however, is something akin to what Marx described as a dictatorship of the proletariat. This would be a world in which, a la Rousseau, private property is banished. No one would own the means of production because no one would own anything. Property would be held in common; hence all would be equal. Each would produce according to his or her abilities and each would receive in accord with his or her needs.

Obviously Marx and Durkheim are at odds. Durkheim seeks a cooperative society by counseling restraint and mutual understanding, whereas Marx seeks justice by advising workers to overthrow their masters. Some conflict theorists go further and accuse the structural-functionalists of denying social change. They claim that an emphasis on passing the traditional division of labor from one generation to the next precludes making adjustments in what is done. Yet this is misleading. The real difference between the two is that the structural-functionalists emphasize evolutionary change, whereas the conflict theorists favor revolutionary transformations.

So which side is right? Which theory better describes society as we know it? Clearly society is less collaborative than Durkheim suggests, but it is equally clear that Marx's predictions have not come true. His proletarian revolution never materialized in advanced capitalist societies, nor have proletarians been reduced to universal misery. Some contemporary conflict theories talk as if poverty is the norm among contemporary workers, but this is obvious hyperbole. All one has to do is drive through modern working-class suburbs to discover that it is an exaggeration.

In fact, the structural-functionalists and the conflict theorists are not as inherently opposed as it often seems. Sociologists often talk as if a person must be one or the other, but this is not true. The structural-functionalists emphasize the importance of social roles in organizing complex societies, and this is the case, whereas the conflict theorists emphasize the significance of social hierarchies, which is also the case. Human beings are both role-playing animals and hierarchical animals. It is not a matter of their being one or the other, but of how these two forms of interaction relate. Sadly, neither of these macro theories does a complete job in explaining how these mechanisms intersect.

THE SMALL PICTURE—MICRO THEORIES

Far and away, the dominant micro sociological theories are variations of symbolic interaction. These theories stress the centrality of symbolic behavior in coordinating the activities of different human beings. To a lesser extent, they also emphasize the role of emotions in harmonizing the actions of separate players. They begin with the notion that people are symbol users—that is, that they utilize signs and emblems to exchange information between one another. Both verbal and nonverbal means are used to communicate data that enable them to act in concert. Individuals can predict what others will do because these others may employ language and/or gestures to indicate what they intend.

Just how special these abilities are can be garnered by comparing human communicative skills with that of any other animal. If one person says to another, "Touch the tip of your nose with the tip of your index finger," the second knows exactly what is desired and can comply.

This is not a matter of training, for if the word "ring" is substituted for "index" the appropriate adjustment will be made. A comparable flexibility is not possible with one's pet dog. It might learn to respond to specific commands, but these could not be altered in the myriad unplanned ways that are possible between human beings who speak the same language.

Consider too the complexity of the information that can be packaged within a few spoken sounds. If one person says to another, "My father was poor but honest," this seems a simple, and easily comprehended, message. But how would one dog communicate this information to another? How would it indicate that "my" is a possessive or that "father" betokens a complex biological and social relationship? And what about "was"? How does a canine indicate past tense? Or "poverty"? Or "honesty"? Indeed, no dog could come close to conveying meanings that people take for granted. It is thus this ability to which symbolic interactionists turn to explicate the multifaceted nature of human cooperative endeavors.

One of the earliest, and still important, symbolic interactionists was Charles Horton Cooley. Among other things, Cooley distinguished between primary and secondary groups. The primary groups were those based on close emotional relationships, such as families, whereas secondary ones were less close, such as industrial corporations. But Cooley is best remembered for his notion of the "looking-glass self." In studying his own children, he discovered that their personal identities were forged through interaction with close caregivers. The very ways these youngsters understood themselves were a reflection of how these others treated them.

Imagine a mother holding her infant child. Imagine also that this mother is suffering from postpartum depression. When her child looks up into her eyes, he will see a distant blankness from which he will derive a dismal message. He will conclude—probably not in words, but in a more distressing emotional dialect—that there is something wrong with him. In seeing what is thought to be a reflection of himself in his mother's eyes, he will assume that he is unlovable. As an infant, he will not understand the source of his parent's unhappiness, but will blame it on himself. The likelihood is that this will carry forward, and all his life he will believe himself inadequate for reasons that have nothing to do with his personal characteristics.

Now imagine a different scenario. Imagine a mother who deeply loves her little daughter. Further imagine that this love is visible in the twinkling eyes of the parent. The little girl will surely discern this brightness and she will conclude that she caused it. Now she will feel loved, but more than this, she will feel worthy of love. Should her mother also treat her as beautiful, she will, in addition, come to think of herself as beautiful. This will probably be the case even if others do not share her mother's evaluation. Because children have very limited experience, but also because they are sensitive to the emotional messages emanating from those upon whom they are dependent, they wind up assessing themselves as these others do. It is these messages, and not some more objective truth, that determines how they believe they fit in with others.

Another of the more influential symbolic interactionist thinkers is Erving Goffman. He is noted for putting forth the *dramaturgical* model of human interaction. According to Goffman, Shakespeare got it right. All the world really is a stage and all the men and women are but actors on this platform. Each is regularly engaged in broadcasting performances intended to influence the way others perceive them. The way they talk, the manner in which they dress, and the props they carry around communicate how they wish to be regarded. Symbols may also be used to manipulate others into behaving the way a person desires.

Goffman talked about the "presentation of self in everyday life." He might observe, for instance, that a banker dresses the way he does because he wishes to create a particular impression. Bankers have long been noted for their dreary, uptight costumes. Pin-stripe suits with expensive ties have virtually been the uniform of their vocation. Some may dismiss this as a reflection of their boring personalities, but a better explanation derives from the needs of their job. Bankers have to be trustworthy. Patrons would not trust them with their money if they did not believe their funds would be safe. Boring, well-tailored clothing proclaims that the wearer is under control and too conventional to become an embezzler. Hippie-style clothing, on the other hand, would convey no such connotation.

The same considerations apply when a person is preparing for a job interview. In this case it is important to arrive on time and to be well groomed. To do otherwise suggests a lack of reliability. Similarly, when going out on a first date, it is a good idea to take a shower before heading out. When one arrives at the date's home, it would be a bad idea to wipe one's nose on one's sleeve or to scratch one's derriere in the presence of her father. It would be an even worse idea to express in words one's sexual intentions for the prospective encounter. The goal is instead to give the impression that one is an upstanding person and a desirable catch.

Another of Goffman's contributions was the distinction between front-stage and backstage behavior. While doing research at a hotel in northern Scotland, he became aware that the waiters and waitresses acted very differently depending upon whether they were in the kitchen or out in the dining area. When out among the patrons they tended to stand up straight and be very polite. When back in the kitchen, however, that is, when backstage where the customers could not see them, their comportment was utterly different. Not only did they slouch, but they made insulting references to the very persons over whom they had previously been fawning. No longer having to communicate messages to audiences that might reward them with tips, they could dispense with their front-stage act.

This same distinction can also explain behavior in other locales. It makes sense of why we may walk around dishabille in our bedrooms early on a Sunday morning, but if the front door bell rings, we quickly cover ourselves with a robe. It also explains how we prepare to give a party. Before our guests arrive and turn what had been backstage into front, we clean the dishes in the sink and straighten up the bathroom. We do not want our friends to perceive us disorganized slobs, but as congenial hosts who are respectful of their sensibilities. In a sense, we are manipulating symbols to convince them that we live in a manner that we do not. But this is one of the glories of symbols. They not only communicate truths, but also convenient fictions.

Symbolic interaction may not explain all micro-level interactions, but it nevertheless clearly makes sense of a great many. The perspective is also compatible with both structural-functionalist and conflict theories. Role behaviors and hierarchical arrangements are both subject to symbolic manipulation. Words and gestures enable people to communicate the sorts of behaviors they expect from their role partners, as well as to indicate the dominance and/or submission that are a regular part of hierarchical relationships.

Questions

1. How do people behave in public places other than elevators—places such as public bathrooms?
2. What are your own social biases, and how do you handle disagreements with others who have opposing biases?

3. Who comes closer to the truth—Durkheim or Marx?

4. What sorts of impressions do you seek to leave—and in what circumstances?

Selected Readings

Durkheim, E. 1933. *The Division of Labor in Society.* New York: The Free Press.

Goffman, E. 1959. *The Presentation of Self in Everyday Life.* Garden City: Doubleday and Co.

Lofland, J. 1971. *Analyzing Social Settings.* Belmont, CA: Wadsworth Publishing Co.

Marx, K., and Engels, F. 1935 [1848]. "The Communist Manifesto." *In Selected Works.* London: Lawrence and Wishart.

3

Social Domains:
Culture and Structure

ETHNOCENTRISM

Not only do people live within communities with other people, but they live within particular communities. Every one of us grows up at a specific time and place. This means that we grow up with particular people who have specific ways of doing things. The human groups in which we are situated always have unique cultures and structures. The ways of life in which we are embedded and the relationships in which we are enmeshed are therefore not generalized, nor are they formless. Rather, they are distinctive, and just as significant, they differ from the cultures and structures present in other communities.

Every society has a unique culture and structure. Indeed, there is no such thing as a society without a distinctive culture or structure. But what is a culture or a social structure? These concepts have become critical to describing the subject matter of the social sciences, but what do they designate? Nowadays "culture" has plainly become a familiar idea. Most people understand that the idea is no longer limited to high culture—that is, that it now refers to something besides the opera, the ballet, or the fine arts. They realize that it has something to do with the way people live; yet most would be hard-pressed to be more exact.

In fact, social scientists themselves do not agree on a precise definition. For most of them, culture includes the fine arts, but also moral rules, scientific beliefs, technological innovations, and interpersonal values. The lists that anthropologists and sociologists have compiled contain many of these social domains, but perhaps the simplest way to delineate what culture means is to describe it as "a learned and shared way of life." In other words, culture is not specific to any particular individual. It is, rather, a conventionalized lifestyle present within a community that is passed along from one generation to the next. Individuals may help modify this culture, but they do not create it out of whole cloth.

This definition does not completely delineate culture, but for the moment let us move on to social structure. Actually, in clarifying this latter concept, we will also illuminate the former. Social structure has to do with interpersonal relationships. It refers to enduring patterns of such relationships. It indicates who interacts with whom, and in what ways they do so. A family would therefore count as a social structure, as would an industrial corporation. These structures are characterized by the positions individuals hold, not by the individuals themselves. Thus, a professional baseball team will have pitchers and outfielders, and can remain the same team even though the individuals filling these roles change with each new season.

Every society is therefore typified by relatively stable ways of life and relatively secure patterns of interpersonal dealings. Moreover, these cultures and structures are in constant interaction. Cultural directives may indicate with whom a person is supposed to perform particular actions, whereas these persons, in turn, demand certain sorts of behaviors. It is never the case that either culture or structure is present in isolation. Perhaps the simplest way to think of these is to assert that culture defines how people should act, whereas structure indicates with whom they should perform these activities.

What can happen when a culture and/or structure falls apart was not long ago demonstrated among the Ik, a tribe in northern Kenya. As documented by anthropologist Colin Turnbull, their traditional ways of life were thoroughly disrupted by the nation's central government. In an effort to establish a national park, the Ik were removed from their home territory and moved into unfamiliar terrain. Although historically hunter-gatherers, they were asked to farm a piece of land ravaged by drought. Sadly, in short order, they found themselves incapable of supporting themselves and struggled to survive.

So bad did conditions become that parents, in order to save themselves, cast out three-year-old children and required them to scrounge food on their own. Outsiders who encountered the Ik during this period considered them mean-spirited. Yet the problem was much worse than this. Almost every society has rules requiring parents to raise and protect their children, as the Ik did when they occupied their original homeland. But environmental stress made it impossible for them to honor these standards. Instead, they became normless. They suffered from what Durkheim called *anomie*. In this culturally bereft situation, their social structure also suffered. The time-honored bonds between parents and their children were stretched to the breaking point, which further eroded their established culture by making it virtually impossible for parents to pass this along to their young.

Without a doubt, this is an extreme case. Few societies are so violently uprooted as were the Ik. In most cases, cultures and structures are so durable that those embedded in them assume that they are both normal and eternal. The ways they live and the patterns of interaction in which they take part appear to be the correct ways of living and interacting. From where they sit, there does not seem to be a reasonable alternative. Others who do not share these patterns are therefore likely to be regarded as less than human. They are also perceived as vaguely immoral.

This phenomenon, this disposition to regard one's own ways as best, is usually referred to as ethnocentrism. People tend to believe that their own community is at the center of the universe and that they are the only genuine people in the cosmos. All others, because they seem strange, are viewed with suspicion. They may thus be treated as culturally defective and excluded from the innermost relationships of one's community. They will, in short, be dealt with as outcasts precisely because they are different.

Ethnocentrism is practically universal. Moreover, it takes many forms. Ponder the name of the peoples who live near the North Pole, the ones who inhabit igloos. When asked their name, most of us will reply "Eskimos." But these peoples do not call themselves Eskimos— they refer to themselves as the Inuit. "Eskimo," it seems, is a Cree Indian word. In the language of these southern neighbors of the Inuit, it means "blubber eaters." Yet who would refer to themselves as blubber eaters? No, the Inuit call themselves Inuit because in their language this means "the people." In essence, they think of themselves as the only fully human beings there are.

Moving over a thousand miles to the south, one encounters an Amerindian tribe usually designated the "Sioux." But the Sioux don't call themselves the "Sioux." This is a word adopted by their neighbors that signifies "the enemy." Obviously, this description would not work within the Sioux community. No, they call themselves the Lakota, which, not surprisingly, in their language means "the people." They too think of themselves as the center of the universe and as the one real people. In this, they are joined by the Jews, who consider themselves God's "chosen people," and African Americans, who claim to have "soul," ostensibly in contrast with other peoples who do not.

Traveling out of North America and into Europe, one stumbles upon the Mediterranean Sea. The Romans sometimes referred to this body of water as *Mare Nostrum,* which means "our sea," but it is the denotation "Mediterranean" that is most instructive. Its literal meaning is "the middle of the earth." The Romans thus thought of themselves as living at the center of the earth. But so did the Chinese. The traditional designation for their country was "the Middle Kingdom." If this seems a trifle self-centered, should one consult a world map printed in America, it places the United States at the center even though this requires slicing Eurasia in half. Japanese maps, conversely, place Japan in the middle.

The ancient Greeks went so far as to refer to non-Greek speakers as barbarians. This derived from their impression that these others did not possess a truly human language, but only made peculiar noises that sounded like "ba-ba-ba." The point is that we all see things from our own perspective. The cultures and structures with which we grow up are familiar and natural in ways that others are not. Of late, it has become conventional to disparage this tendency and to exhort people to think in more universal terms. But this is not in the cards. Because ethnocentrism has its origins in the parochialism of childhood, it cannot be expunged at the moment it is established. Beginning from a limited life space, we, of necessity, interpret what we see in terms of the materials at hand.

What can happen, however, is that some individuals will move beyond ethnocentrism as they mature. In the process of growing out of childhood, they are exposed to a wider social circle. If they allow themselves to do so, they thereby discover that other people, people they never met when they were small, really are human even though their ways of life and patterns of interaction differ from their own. Culture and structure make a difference, but they do not trump our underlying humanity. In fact, becoming more cosmopolitan can alter our own ways of living. This is perhaps the best demonstration that our humanity and lifestyles are not synonymous.

RELATIVISM

Closely related to the notion of ethnocentrism is that of relativism. Social scientists, because they have discovered that cultures and structures are at least in part socially constructed, have concluded that these are relative to the communities that assemble them. They tell us that what is true within one society is true for it, irrespective of what other societies may believe. This, unfortunately, conceals a serious confusion. It muddles two types of relativism—two sorts of understanding that have different implications.

The first sort of relativism may be called *cultural relativism.* This concept derives from the experiences of anthropologists. As they traveled around the globe to study obscure tribal communities, they were struck by the humanity of their disparate subjects. People might dress, eat, and speak differently, but these diverse designs usually made sense within their respective environments. Most societies were intelligently coping with the challenges unique to their situation. It was therefore crucial to understand what they were doing from their point of view. A failure to make this shift in perspective made it impossible to comprehend what was really occurring.

The classic instance of this is the Indian attitude toward cattle. These beasts were regarded as sacred and therefore taboo to consume. Westerners, upon perceiving this custom, initially perceived it as irrational. Why not eat cows, especially during periods of famine? Wouldn't this save countless millions of lives? What these observers did not recognize, because they were not viewing it from the Indian point of view, is that the Indian subcontinent is dependent upon monsoons to support its agriculture. The rains come only during certain seasons and must be taken advantage of when they appear.

But the monsoons do not always arrive on schedule. In years when the El Niño pattern affects oceanic currents, there may be no nourishing rains. At such times, there may be a terrible famine; hence the temptation to consume one's oxen can be great. Yet Indian cattle are draft animals. They pull the plows that allow the farmers to cultivate their fields. If they were to slaughter these beasts during periods of want, they would not be available to perform this essential chore. The result would be even greater famine when the rains returned. Maintaining the religious prohibition against consuming cows is therefore sensible. In the long run, it preserves more lives than would the recommendations of those ignorant of local conditions.

Cultural relativism is thus fundamental to social science. An inability to see things from the perspective of those studied would be tantamount to closing one's eyes to critical facts. It would be to allow one's biases to blind one to the subject matter one is attempting to understand. The dangers of taking this tack became apparent during the colonial era, when European administrators disregarded native customs at their peril. In one notable case the British rulers of India helped precipitate a mutiny among the indigenous troops—that is, the Sepoys—by failing to understand that Muslims would be outraged by being asked to bite into bullets lubricated by pig grease, while Hindus would feel the same about cartridges smeared with beef fat. In our contemporary society, government agents often make similar errors when dealing with the family arrangements of recent immigrants. They may thus mistake customary parent-child interactions as abusive, when they are not.

Cultural relativism is consequently valid, whereas ethical relativism may not be. Ethical relativism is about moral judgments, not about seeing things from the perspectives of others. It asserts that because moral rules are socially constructed, whatever a particular society declares to be right is correct for that society. Outsiders do not have a right to criticize a society's customs because the appropriate standards of judgment exist only within the affected community. Thus, if the Aztecs killed thousands of captives by cutting their still-beating hearts out of their chests, this was right for them. Their belief that it was necessary to feed the God's blood if the sun was to shine and the rains to fall justified this sanguinary practice. Likewise, if migrants to the United States believe in enforcing arranged marriages, this is suitable for them. The issue is respecting diversity, rather than imposing ethnocentrism.

But what would these same ethical relativists say about the holocaust? Would they assert that because the Nazis believed that the Jews and Slavs were less human than Aryans, they had a right to slaughter twelve million of them in their concentration camps? And what about slavery? Would they accept the proposition that slavery was morally acceptable in the antebellum American South because most Southerners defined it as moral? And how about what has been called female circumcision? In many areas of the world it is considered essential to excise the clitoris and/or the labia of small girls. Is this morally justifiable, or is it a form of genital mutilation?

Clearly, those who promote ethical relativism are faced with a quandary. There would seem to be many instances where they too would want to interfere with customary practices. In fact, they need not fret. The proposition that one should not judge other societies is itself a moral injunction. As such, it is no more (or less) valid than other moral prescriptions. It does not float outside societies, enjoining them not to meddle with one another. Indeed, societies regularly trod on each other's turf. And when they do, they may influence each other's beliefs. This is what occurred when the British colonized New Guinea. They were scandalized by the local practice of cannibalism and hence banned it. The natives at first resisted, but in time they came to agree with the British. Forced by these outsiders to change their behaviors, their attitudes were eventually modified as well.

CULTURAL DOMAINS

The time has now come to be specific about the kinds of life encompassed by particular cultures. What sorts of behaviors are learned and shared within particular communities? What ways of dealing with the world and with other people are transmitted through the generations? There are a variety of these, several of which are critical to understanding how any given society operates. The first of these is the *social norm*. A norm is a social rule, a rule that is sanctioned by a particular group. These sanctions may be rewards or punishments, or a combination of both. In either case, the violation of a norm is met with resistance.

Let us begin with an example. Imagine that a college professor saunters into his classroom wiping his brow. He then starts unbuttoning the top button of his shirt. At this, he asks his class if they would mind his removing his shirt because he is feeling warm. Before he finishes, however, he inquires if it would be okay to remove his trousers as well because they are beginning to bind. How do you think the class would react? Would they simply accept this as his prerogative? Would they continue going about their normal classroom routine? Not likely!

What would probably happen is this. At first the students would become nervous. This performance is not what they expect in a college classroom. They would, as a result, begin squirming in their seats and then glancing around at each other. With their eyes they would ask each other if they are actually seeing what they thought they were seeing. They would, in essence, be requesting validation for their impression that what was occurring was socially unacceptable. Upon perceiving each other's discomfort they would realize that they were witnessing a norm violation, and many would become indignant. Some might even stomp out of the room to complain to the dean. The dean would then, in all likelihood, call in the professor to inform him that his services were no longer necessary. In this case, an initially informal sanction would have escalated to a significant formal sanction. The professor would have learned that even unspoken rules carry enormous penalties.

Let us now shift our focus to the students. Assume that the professor asks one of the students sitting in the middle of the room to turn her chair around so that she is facing the back. How would she react? Mind you, she will have been visibly asked to break an informal rule by her professor. Would this make a difference? Probably not. She would still feel uncomfortable and be eager to turn back in the "proper" direction. One reason for her discomfort would be the disapproving faces of the students surrounding her. Even though these scholars too were given to understand this as a classroom exercise, they would be hard pressed to squelch their condemnation. It would be perceptible in their eyes and body postures.

In the United States children grow up being told that they live in a free country. Many assume that this means they can do whatever they like—that they are at liberty to behave as they wish. But this is not true. As in any human community, they are surrounded by a palisade of norms that limit their options. All of us are encircled by friends, relatives, and perfect strangers who, through word and gesture, are prepared to inform us when we overstep the bounds. If we were, for instance, to grasp the handle of a soup spoon with our fist, instead of our first three fingers, they would frown in disgust and we would soon discover that there is a socially prescribed way to eat soup. We are not allowed to imbibe it any way we please.

Sociologists distinguish between several sorts of norms. One type is the *folkway*. These are social rules that are moderately enforced. They concern things like the clothes people wear or the language they employ. Thus, if a person chooses to dye her hair green, she will meet disapproving eyes, but she will not be thrown in jail. She may be considered strange, but not immoral. If, however, she murders someone, the situation is entirely different. In this case, she will have violated a *more*. Now the sanctions will escalate. Instead of others being bemused, they will be outraged. Finally, some norms are formalized and governmentally enforced. They are codified into *laws* and violators are pursued by the police, adjudicated in the courts, and punished in prisons.

It is also essential to recognize that these norms vary from community to community and from era to era. In the play the *Music Man*, pool players using the word "swell" scandalize the town's people. The term is considered vulgar and a sign of delinquency. We, of course, are amused by this reaction, as we are by nineteenth-century inhibitions about showing a woman's ankle in public. Nowadays, of course, community standards vary with respect to homosexual behavior, religious beliefs, and public nudity. Not every group is prepared to enforce the same practices. To know which norms count as norms, one must understand the consensus present within the particular community.

A second critical aspect of culture has to do with *values*. What people consider important also varies from community to community. These judgments also are learned and passed down through the generations. If norms stipulate how people should behave, values inform them about the goals they are supposed to pursue. Though it is true that some goals are a matter of personal taste—for example, some people prefer chocolate to vanilla ice cream—much of what we desire is determined by what we are taught is desirable. The community holds up some aims as superior to others and applauds their achievement.

In contemporary America, it has become the custom for women who are engaged to be given an engagement ring. This piece of jewelry is typically a diamond ring. Diamonds, it needs to be admitted, are quite attractive. But it must also be admitted that they are merely pieces of stone. Why then all the fuss? Why are most women reluctant to give up their diamonds in favor of large pieces of quartz? Quartz is also attractive and can be obtained in huge blocks. Or why not exchange a diamond for a ballpoint pen? After all, a pen can write messages, whereas all diamonds do is look pretty.

When asked why they are attached to their diamonds, most women claim that they have sentimental value. But couldn't they get similarly attached to ballpoint pens? If they owned them long enough and wrote sentimental letters with them, why not? Surprisingly, diamond engagement rings are of recent vintage. Golden wedding rings, in contrast, go back to Roman times, but diamonds did not acquire widespread cache until the 1930s. It was at this time that the DeBeers company began to promote them as a way of marketing the product it monopolized. To be blunt, the value of diamond engagement rings was established by an advertising campaign. In persuading people that they were valuable, these items became valuable. DeBeers, of course, is still at it. Today they inform the public that "diamonds are forever." The goal is now to convince people not to sell their diamonds so that their price remains high.

One of the factors that helps shape a social consensus that a specific object is valuable is its relative rarity. Diamonds tend to be favored over quartz because they are comparatively scarce, which is why DeBeers aims to keep things this way. Rarity matters because if there is less of something, then not everyone can have it. Possessing it therefore becomes a sign that one has the power to deprive others of what they too crave. It is visible proof that one is stronger than they are. This is the reason that large houses, fancy cars, and opulent yachts are held in high esteem—not because they are extremely comfortable. It is why caviar is highly valued although most people find it less appetizing than ice cream. It is why silver costs more than aluminum. Oddly, it was once aluminum that was more expensive. Before it could easily be extracted from bauxite, it was scarcer and therefore more desirable.

A third significant aspect of culture is our shared *beliefs*. We human beings belong to cognitive communities. What we consider to be true is often a reflection of what those surrounding us deem to be true. Although we tend to think of ourselves as independent judges of truth, it is amazing how much of what we believe we know has actually been transmitted to us by other people. It is what these others tell us is so, more than what we directly perceive, that is regarded as real.

Let us return to our college classroom where our professor is now expounding upon the cultural nature of personal beliefs. Suddenly in the midst of his disquisition, he turns toward his open briefcase and begins having a private conversation. At this point, he excuses himself and tells the class that he is discussing matters with his personal gnome Herman. Herman, he informs them, is distressed that the class disagrees with what he has been saying. He further asserts that Herman is prepared to punish those who are disrespectful of his friend. The students, meanwhile, look on bemused, not quite sure of what to make of what is occurring.

At this juncture the professor chooses to ask the class if they believe in Herman. Do they think that his gnome is real? Needless to say, most express their doubts. The professor then asks them if they believe in God. This, of course, elicits a very different response. Virtually every person in the class asserts that they do. Why do they believe in one, but not the other? Someone will usually suggest that they have not seen Herman, thus they cannot be sure he is present. Well, retorts the professor, have they seen God? Have they had a "burning bush" experience wherein God has appeared to them in person? Few students claim they have. Most have prayed to God, or concluded that he exists from observing his works, but they have not really observed Him with their own eyes. Well then, why do they believe in Him?

Eventually it becomes plain that religious faith derives from social sources. People believe in God because their parents and ministers have told them that God exists. This is why the children of Baptists tend to be Baptists, whereas the children of Hindus typically become Hindus. Their original sources of their faith possess a degree of authority that the professor lacks, especially since their influence commenced when the students were very young.

This conclusion may appear to be antireligious, but it is not. The same dynamics also apply to science. Scientists tell their students that they can check scientific facts for themselves, but this is not what actually takes place. A high school science teacher may, for instance, claim to demonstrate that hydrogen and oxygen combine to make water by bringing a balloon filled with hydrogen and another filled with oxygen together and then igniting them. But how do the witnesses know what is in these balloons? The answer is that the teacher has told them so. All they actually see are two balloons. The rest depends upon accepting the teacher's authority. The same applies to the atomic theory. Most people today believe that physical objects are composed of atoms, but they do not directly perceive these little bits of matter. They must take the word of the scientists. They similarly accept the testimony of physicians and biologists that germs cause diseases. They don't observe this process for themselves.

This is strong stuff, but our dependence on others for what we believe goes well past religion and science. It also extends into our personal lives. None of us can be everywhere and see everything. How many of us have visited Romania? How, then, can we be sure that there is such a place? We may have seen pictures, but these could have been faked. Perhaps there is a vast conspiracy intent on convincing us there are foreign lands that, in fact, exist only on sound stages—much as some persons believe that the moon landings were staged somewhere in Arizona.

Even in our day-to-day transactions we depend on input from other people. How do we know that Mary is angry at us? Why, because John told us so. But could John have been manipulating symbols in order to deceive us? Perhaps. Nevertheless, we usually take people's word for these things—that is, if we trust them. But mostly, we do trust people. Most of the time we assume that what others communicate to us is true.

How dependent we are on others was confirmed by a classic experiment conducted by social psychologist Solomon Asche. He asked students to indicate which of two lines was longer. But before he did, he arranged for a series of confederates to declare that the longer was in fact the shorter. Given this social context, most of his subjects went along with the crowd. Many even convinced themselves that the longer was shorter. In this situation, they were victims of our need for consensual validation. Before we human beings are prepared to commit ourselves, we generally require the agreement of others that what we believe is true really is the case. Only then are we comfortable that we have got it right.

The last cultural domain we will discuss is *material culture.* As with norms, values, and beliefs, we are dependent upon others for the physical objects with which we manipulate the world. We did not personally invent shoes, chairs, or television sets. Each of these has been transmitted to us via the society of which we are a part. Few of us would consider walking through the woods barefoot, although our remote ancestors probably did. Likewise, few of us sit Indian fashion while eating dinner. Our kindergarten teachers taught us how to emulate Amerindians, but we probably didn't reflect on why the Indians sat this way. It was because as nomads, they did not have chairs. We do, however, and as such we have learned to use them. For us, thanks to our cultural predecessors, this seems natural.

Our material culture, especially our advanced technology, has done much to shape our lifestyles. Items such as the electric light and the automobile have molded our sleeping routines and eating habits. Before Edison perfected the incandescent bulb, people went to bed earlier than nowadays. Similarly, before the automobile few people ate kiwi fruit. Nor did they purchase this produce at supermarkets. Actually, supermarkets could not exist without being able to attract a sizeable clientele. But a large number of customers could not congregate in the same store without the automobile to transport them there from considerable distances. Moreover, to complete the circle, it is only their presence in substantial numbers that makes it profitable to stock kiwi fruits. Automobiles are also the reason we consume so many hamburgers. They are what made fast-food chains, such as McDonald's, practical.

The far-reaching nature of the implications of technology—shaping even our social structures—is evident in events that took place in Australia at the beginning of the twentieth century. Anthropologists engaged in the study of aboriginal culture sought informants among the Yir Yoront. In order to obtain their cooperation, they offered them gifts. Since this tribe was still dependent upon a Neolithic technology, they decided to offer them steel axes. Until this point they had utilized hand-ground stone axes. These were laborious to produce and inferior to steel; hence the new implements were welcome.

What the anthropologists had not considered was the potential impact on tribal relationships. Prior to their arrival, the tribal elders controlled the highly prized stone axes. Others, including women and children, who wished to use them, thus had to defer to these older men. Once steel axes were distributed among even the least powerful members of the community, all this changed. Now women and children could safely ignore the wishes of the former tribal leaders. A mere piece of mechanical equipment turned interpersonal transactions on their head and altered the traditional social structure. A simple tool irredeemably transformed their way of life and their patterns of interaction.

STRUCTURAL DOMAINS

As with culture, there are many different structural patterns that shape human societies. People can relate to each other via personal relationships, hierarchical configurations, and social roles. Some people are treated differently because they are friends or relatives, whereas others are deferred to or dominated because they are of a higher or lower social class, and still others become role partners because what they do fits in with what we do. Each of these structural patterns is essential to how communities sustain themselves and therefore will be dealt with in greater detail in later chapters.

In the meantime, a few words must be tendered to distinguish between these structures. *Personal relationships* are familiar to each of us. We all, for instance, grow up in families. And almost all of us know what it means to be a friend. Part of being human is making distinctions between human beings. Other individuals are not treated as interchangeable. One dollar bill may be as valuable as another, but one person is unlikely be as significant as a second. We are attached to some, but not to others. One person is our lover, whereas another is a stranger. One is our child, whereas a second is part of an anonymous crowd. Moreover, we can tell the difference. Other people do not look the same, nor do we react to them in the same way.

Families are probably the locus of the most easily recognized sort of personal relationship. We readily understand that families tend to be stable over time. Even in this era of divorce, husbands and wives forge bonds that are not easily severed. Open marriages may once have been touted as the wave of the future, but most of us recognize that long-term sexual intimacy is not like a handshake with stranger. Hence we are careful in selecting our mates. Moreover, it makes a great deal of difference whether we have sex with this person rather than that one. More significant still, if our bed partner has indiscriminate sex with others, we are not indifferent. We do not pass off what are called "infidelities" as if they were a matter of biting into one apple rather than another.

We surely do not regard our children as interchangeable. On the contrary, we establish bonds with our offspring that are viewed as sacred. To fail to honor such commitments is universally perceived as disgraceful. A person who sloughed off this sort of relationship would be thought less than human. Even friendships, however, make a difference in the way we behave. When people get to like each other they expect their friends to treat them differently than strangers. They look forward to being invited to dinner; they anticipate being greeted with a smile. Were there a lack of such recognition, or an unwillingness to be helpful, it would elicit displeasure in a way that similar responses from a nonfriend would not.

Hierarchical relationships, as opposed to personal ones, are not always cherished. Individual bonds are generally welcomed, whereas relationships that entail unequal status may not be. But inequality, too, is part of the human experience. People rank themselves relative to each other, with some being regarded as superior and others inferior. Humans habitually establish stable configurations in which the members of these groups understand where they fit compared with others. They may not be fond of the positions they occupy—they may even be intent upon altering them—but they are keenly sensitive to institutionalized differences in power.

Complex organizations, such as corporations, are structured around hierarchical distinctions. The participants understand who is the boss and who is the subordinate. They realize that when one person leaves a position another can be appointed to replace him or her. Indeed, the organization maintains its integrity as an organization by preserving its overall hierarchical arrangements. It is these that provide its continuity and internal discipline. Hierarchies may not be loved, but they provide the scaffolding of many social interactions.

Hierarchical relations are also at the base of larger social arrangements. All modern mass-societies incorporate social class relations. People sometimes talk about everyone being equal, but when they are candid, they recognize that this is not so. They say that everyone puts on their pants one leg at a time, but when someone from a higher social class enters their space, they are deferential. They are more polite than they would be with their peers, and though perhaps resentful of this inferiority, keep to their station. Karl Marx considered social class an abomination that was destined to be cast on the ash heap of history, but that day has not yet arrived. We may live in a democracy, but it is not a democracy in which everyone commands the same prestige as everyone else.

Last, all societies are divided into *social roles.* Durkheim made this abundantly plain when he alluded to a social division of labor. People do not all perform the same jobs. They have different specialties. Some are butchers; some are bakers; some are candlestick makers. When they approach each other in the marketplace, what they demand of each other depends upon their perceived positions. One does not go to the butcher to purchase a loaf of bread. So well understood are these occupational roles that when people are asked to identify themselves, they often mention these niches. They tell people at a party, "I am a doctor," or "I am a college professor."

Nevertheless, certain other roles are less well recognized. Many of these are personal, as opposed to occupational, roles. Some are associated with our membership in families. We are husbands and wives, mothers and fathers, sisters and brothers. These derive from our biological and/or personal relationships. One of the primary personal roles is the gender role. When we are born, the first question is generally: What is it? The expected answer is either a *boy* or a *girl*. Recently, feminism has made this sort of identification suspect, yet it remains fundamental to how most people regard themselves and are regarded by others. The ways we talk, the ways we walk, and the manners in which we dress are all influenced by gender roles. Transsexuals discover this in the process of transforming from one gender into the other. They quickly learn that behaving as the other sex does is more difficult than they supposed, but also that others will relate to them in a significantly different manner. If nowhere else, they discover this when they choose a public lavatory.

There is another sort of personal role that has as much impact. Such roles may be called "basic" roles, in that they are typically established early in life and provide a foundation for later roles. Sometimes confused with personal traits, they are in fact a derivative of family-based divisions of labor. Suppose that a son is born into a family. Suppose further that he is a bright little boy. Intelligence is to a large extent biologically inherited, but how he will be treated is not. Suppose now that his parents are proud of his intelligence and prompt him to show off whenever relatives come to visit. He will, in this case, be well on the way to developing the role of the "intelligent one" in the family.

Now suppose that a girl is born into the family. Suppose further that she is less intelligent than the boy, but that she is a very active child. She may soon acquire the reputation for being the athlete in the family. Compared with her brother she will be the stupid one, whereas compared with her, he will be the klutz. Since these is room for only one smartest and one most athletic, once these slots are filled, the other is consigned to the opposite. These attributions then become settled facts and both he and she will continue to regard themselves this way and to make life choices based on this role identity. In fact, she may be very smart and capable of more demanding tasks than she knows, while he may be much more nimble than he is aware of and suited to more physical endeavors than he ever attempts.

Other personal roles can be more debilitating. Take the role of scapegoat. In some families, one of the children is singled out to receive the blame for anything that goes wrong. He serves as a sort of lightning rod to protect others from having to confront their failures. Or take the role of caregiver. Sometimes a child will be appointed as the one who is responsible for providing services for other family members. She may then grow up believing that this is her job with respect to everyone else. She may be convinced that her sole value to others lies in keeping them happy. In alcoholic families, on the other hand, it is not unusual for one of the children to be designated the "family hero." The hero's role, in this instance, is to protect others from their weaknesses.

Another distinction that must be made between roles is whether they are ascribed or achieved. Ascribed roles are simply attributed to people because of their biology and/or social station. For example, gender roles are typically ascribed. One does not have to do anything, except have the appropriate genitals, in order to receive this designation. Being a prince is also ascribed. Simply being the first-born son of a king brings this denomination. Becoming a professor of sociology, however, is another matter. Here one has to do something in order to obtain the honor. One has to go to college and obtain grades sufficient to gain acceptance to a graduate school. One must next be hired by a college and ultimately obtain tenure. These are achievements. They entail socialization and accomplishment, not merely being in the right place at the right time.

Finally, it must also be noted that roles tend to come in pairs. These are called *role partnerships*. Husbands go with wives. Indeed, to be a husband one must first have a wife. Similarly, mothers have children and children have mothers. As a matter of fact, to be a mother one must have at least one child. Likewise teachers have students and students have teachers. These tasks are interdependent; hence to be a teacher who does not have students, is not to be a teacher. One might be able to lecture to the trees in a forest, but this is not the same as being a bona fide educator.

SOCIALIZATION

More than anything else, peoplization entails internalizing a community's culture and obtaining positions within its social structure. To be fully human, one must be integrated into a particular group. One must learn how members of the group do things and how they relate to one another. Beyond this, one must be able to behave in the accepted ways with the expected individuals. Frequently a distinction is made between nature and nurture. Nature refers to our biological heritage, whereas nurture refers to our cultural and structural heritage. Though all human beings have both, and it is often useful to determine which is most responsible for particular outcomes, nurture entails socialization. It involves the various ways in which individuals are recruited into the societies of which they are a part.

Sometimes socialization is intentional. In this case it is deliberately structured so as to inculcate desired lessons. This is called *formal socialization* and nowadays is centered around educational institutions. But there is also *informal socialization*. This is comprised of unintended lessons that are imparted in unofficial locations. Informal socialization might seem to be less important than the formal variety, but the opposite is true. The informal sort is much more pervasive and involves basic lessons, such as how to perform one's gender roles. It begins in infancy with the manner in which our parents hold us, continues through the playgroups of early childhood, is present in the families that we establish and the vocations we choose, and culminates in the retirement activities of old age.

The most important purveyors of informal socialization are our role partners. They are the ones who inform us if we are behaving as we should and they are the ones who shape our social performances. Consider how students learn to be students. While attending school they have formal lessons, but they are also exposed to informal ones. Sometimes teachers help them learn how to count, but at other times they tell them to sit up straight or to face the front of the room. These latter lessons, though not found in the curriculum, are essential to how the students comport themselves when they eventually enter a college classroom. By the same token, teachers learn much of what it means to be a competent teacher by responding to the input of their students. Thus, they discover which teaching styles work, and which don't, by monitoring the eyes of their pupils. When students are bored, they telegraph the message that their teacher is doing something wrong and needs to come up with an alternative strategy.

Parallel considerations apply in the home. It is primarily husbands who teach wives how to be wives, and conversely wives who teach husbands how to be husbands. When he becomes distressed at her disparaging remarks, or she bridles at his unwarranted demands, these responses influence the future behavior of their respective partners. Marital socialization may not be their intent, but it is the consequence. In the same way, parents teach their children how to be children, but, more surprisingly, children teach their parents how to be parents. Parents surely inform their children as to what constitutes satisfactory behavior, but children, in what they accept and what they resist, instruct their parents on how to impose discipline. The learning is a two-way street.

Which brings us to a mystery. Socialization has always been part of the peoplization process, but how it has occurred has changed in recent times. The question is: Why is this so? Why have the techniques for recruiting children into the social world undergone dramatic transformations when the fundamental requirements, and the means of socialization, would seem not to have transformed that much?

Reflect on what has happened to the way children are disciplined. When this author was a small boy his father chastised him with a strap. This was a flat belt from which the buckle was removed. When as a boy he cried at this treatment, his grandfather would chuckle. "Why, when I was a boy," he would say, "my father used a cat-o'-nine-tails. We were tough back then; we didn't cry." Nowadays, of course, most youngsters do not even know what a cat-o'-nine-tails is. They have never encountered this small whip with nine leather thongs, each of which is tied in a knot at the end—and have never been subjected to it. Many have never even encountered the strap. Whereas corporal punishment was once considered normal, today it is often regarded as abusive.

In the old days it was said that if one spared the rod, one spoiled the child. Parents were additionally instructed to beat the devil out of their children, and this was meant literally. At the same time, at school the order of the day was reading and writing taught to the tune of the hickory stick. Students would have their knuckles whacked for misbehaving or would be sent to the principal's office to have their derrieres introduced to the board of education. Having to sit in the corner with a dunce cap atop one's head was deemed a mild punishment. All in all, conventional wisdom had it that children should be seen and not heard. It would have been considered absurd, as not long ago occurred at a northern Georgia supermarket, that the police would be called when a mother smacked the bottom of a disobedient son. Today anything but a word of admonition, or a time-out in one's room, is considered excessive.

There have also been other changes in the way children are raised. Once it was common for the offspring, of at least the upper classes, to be put out to be nurtured by wet nurses. In the past, most babies were also tightly wrapped up in swaddling clothes during their first year. Their arms and legs were tightly bound in blankets to prevent them from getting into trouble. Furthermore, children were once dressed in clothing very similar to that of their parents, and played games similar to those played by adults.

More fundamentally, educational requirements have changed. Throughout most of history, children in the Western world underwent apprenticeships. They would be sent to live in the households of individuals who would teach them the trade they would later occupy. They would learn to become blacksmiths by working for blacksmiths, or printers by working in a print shop. This was the fate of most people, including individuals as prominent as Benjamin Franklin. Mandatory grammar school was not initiated until about two hundred years ago.

Compulsory high school is less than a century old. Regular college education has less than a half-century pedigree.

Remarkably, the notion of teenager did not get established until a significant number of persons in their teen years started going to high school. Until then most persons of this age worked ordinary jobs alongside adults and hence interacted with them and not their age peers. It was high school that threw teenagers together and created a distinctive teenage culture. It was then—largely during the 1920s—that they began wearing raccoon coats and singing boola-boola. It was then that a mania for sports, such as football, took hold.

So what has happened? Why have these modifications in childhood socialization occurred more or less in tandem? What, if anything, do they have in common? The answer will have to wait till the next chapter.

Questions

1. Is ethical relativism valid? If it is not, do you believe that there are absolute moral standards?
2. Do you have any distinctive beliefs that derive from your social background? What gives you confidence in them?
3. What personal roles do you occupy? Do they feel comfortable?
4. Were you subjected to corporal punishment when you were young? Was it effective? Do you believe in its use?

Selected Readings

Fein, M. 1990. *Role Change: A Resocialization Perspective*. New York: Praeger.

Harrison, L. E., and Huntington, S. P. (Eds.) 2000. *Culture Matters: How Values Shape Human Progress*. New York: Basic Books.

Norris, C. 1997. *Against Relativism: Philosophy of Science, Deconstruction and Critical Theory*. Oxford, UK: Blackwell Publishers.

Ravitch, D. 2000. *Left Back: A Century of Failed School Reforms*. New York: Simon & Schuster.

Turnbull, C. 1972. *The Mountain Peopler*. New York: Simon & Schuster.

A Hierarchical Animal: Class Consciousness and Inequality

ON BEING THE BEST

Who does not want to be the best? Who does not want to be special? We may not have anything against other people, but would we really want to be at the bottom of the heap? People used to talk about keeping up with the Joneses, and this admittedly sounds a bit crass, but would it really be okay with us to have less than everyone else? Would it be acceptable to us to be losers? Would it be tolerable to be regarded as inferior to other people?

In contemporary America, it is often regarded as a faux pas to endorse anything other than complete equality. No one is supposed to be better than anyone else. Anything other than total parity seems antidemocratic. To be too competitive is deemed to be mean-spirited; it is to lack compassion and to be reluctant to engage in cooperative activities. And yet if we look at the way people actually behave, their actions seem to belie these ideals. Contemporary Americans are quite competitive; they very much desire to beat others. Far from accepting losses with equanimity, as per General George Patton, most are determined to be winners.

Go to virtually any sports venue and there is something you will never observe. You will never encounter a gaggle of fans rooting for their team by chanting "We are number six." No, what they will be chanting is: "We are number one!" Whether their team is winning or not, they aspire to be first. At the very least, they loath the idea of being last. Ask one of the players on the field what motivates him most and he will probably tell you that it is the fear of being the goat. He would certainly be pleased to be the hero of the game, but to be held responsible for a loss would be excruciating. Most of us feel the same way. Whatever happens, we don't want to be last.

We human beings are naturally competitive. We revel in being better than others. As a result, we are forever comparing ourselves with those around us. We want to know who is taller or shorter, who is heavier or thinner, who is lighter or darker. We rank ourselves as to athleticism, beauty, wealth, intelligence, political talent, artistic ability, fashion sense, or just about anything else you can think of. Indeed, we invent sports in order to determine who is best at throwing a ball through a hoop or which automobile (or horse) will arrive at a finish line first. Even little things, such as a superior capacity to drink beer, matter to us.

Some people claim that they hate this obsession with ranking. They urge us all to be friends and to be sensitive to each other's needs. Some women even assert that it is more important for them to find a sensitive man than a competitive one. But when has one chanced upon a woman who contended that she was seeking a nice, sensitive loser? Being nice may be important, yet we human beings are hierarchical animals. For better or worse, we are *all* hierarchical animals. Every one of us hates to lose and we all want to be thought well of. We may not have a need to be best; nevertheless we want to rank as high as we can.

Those at the top of the pyramid did not invent hierarchy. They did not impose an artificial grading system on others in order to force them into defeat. Those at the bottom of the heap also want to be winners. They also compare themselves with others in the hope that they will prove the better. Losing, it is true, hurts. But a desire to win is so ingrained in what it is to be human that we tolerate the pain of loss, even though the collateral distress can be significant—how significant, we will shortly see.

ANIMAL HIERARCHIES

Other animals also have hierarchies. They too also rank themselves in order of dominance. Indeed, most large social animals exhibit these arrangements. But we need to be more concrete. "Big Red" was the beneficiary of one of these chains of command. He was a pigeon who lived on a rooftop in Brooklyn some years ago. A member of a flock of some forty birds, he was their unquestioned master. What ethologists would call an alpha animal, he strode across the roof as if he owned it. If another animal inadvertently crossed his path, it would receive a firm peck on the head and then dash for shelter. No bird was safe from Big Red. Any one of them could be the target of his displeasure at any moment. But he was completely safe from them. Never, not even once, did any of them attempt to peck him.

Big Red was part of a pecking order. Indeed, he stood atop this order. But some of the birds he pecked were also dominant. They never pecked at him, but if he took a whack at them, they immediately rushed off to peck a lesser bird. As betas, they were free to deliver blows to gammas and omegas with immunity. The gammas could then attack the omegas, who, because there were no birds below them, had to absorb violence from every direction. This sequence also had advantages for those at its apex. Thus when their human owners threw seed onto the roof, Big Red was first to eat. No one challenged him as he marched into the seed field to consume his fill. Next came the betas and then the gammas. The omegas, to their chagrin, had to wait their turn and hope for leftovers.

The same pattern applied to the nesting box. Big Red got his choice of nesting squares. He and his mate settled into one toward the center of the matrix, but they also maintained a series of empty holes around them. As might be expected, the betas got the next most favorable sites, and the gammas took the remaining spaces. The omegas typically were shut out. This meant that they were excluded from mating. Not only did they get less food, but they had a lesser chance of reproducing. This may sound unfair—and it was—but the situation was worse than this. It was literally a matter of life and death. Each day, the flock's owners, before they did anything else, inspected the birds for bald spots. Areas without feathers would regularly develop on the omega birds where they had previously been pecked. These would then serve as targets for Big Red and the betas. If some tar were not placed on these patches, the higher-ranking birds would continue to peck at these until the victim was dead.

A similar sort of pattern can be found among baboons. They, to be sure, do not peck each other—they do not have beaks—but they exhibit an equivalent technique for underscoring relative status. These animals are frequently found on the savannahs of East Africa, which are fairly flat planes studded with copses of trees. The baboons are therefore ground dwellers, at least during the day. They usually sit around digging for roots and such. Under these circumstances, when an alpha male wishes to assert his dominance, he may choose to approach a beta to drive him off the patch of ground where he is sitting. To do so, he saunters over, opens his mouth to show his huge canine teeth, and then bats his eyelids. This is generally sufficient to motivate the beta to move on without a fight. The beta then seeks out a gamma to demonstrate his relative dominance. In this way the pecking order is reaffirmed without blood being shed.

The question then arises as to how the alpha male gets to be an alpha in the first place. The answer is that he must win a *test of strength*. He must demonstrate in a physical contest that he is more powerful than another male. Tests of this sort are a standard mechanism for establishing comparative superiority. Among baboons these confrontations can be savage. Thanks to their canines, they can even be lethal. The loser is frequently badly mauled, and if he was the reigning alpha, he may be driven from the troop. What makes baboons less like pigeons and more like people is that prospective alphas frequently seek allies before they launch a challenge. An ambitious beta may curry the favor of another beta by grooming his fur in the hope that when he needs help, his friend will come to augment his power. If their dual effort succeeds, the leader will be the new alpha and his partner will become a beta with privileges.

As with pigeons, high-status baboons eat better, have a better chance of mating, and lead more secure lives. Omegas, on the other hand, live in constant anxiety. They are so apprehensive that they are prone to ulcers. There is also the matter that high status is to some degree inherited. The children of alpha mothers have an advantage over the youngsters of lower-ranking females. If they get into a squabble with other youngsters, they can call on their mothers for assistance. These females, because they are alphas, can provide this without fear of reprisals from beta mothers. Their offspring therefore come to believe that they are superior to their less-well-connected peers. This supplies them with the confidence that may one day give them an edge in tests of strength with rival adults.

By now these patterns should strike a familiar chord. They are not so different from what one encounters among human beings. People too have hierarchies based on comparative power, and they too derive benefits from being at the top of these ranking systems. People also exploit alliances to get ahead and benefit from being born into the right family. William Foote Whyte drove home just how close these parallels are in a classic piece of research. Just prior to World War II he conducted a participant observation study of a street gang in Boston. He hung around with these late adolescent early adult Italian boys seeking to understand how they were organized. His subsequent book, *Street Corner Society*, became a masterpiece of ethnography.

The leader of the gang was called Doc. A good politician and a competent mediator, he was able to maintain alliances with most of the members of his group. As such, his opinions were respected and his dominance was valued. When Whyte inquired as to how Doc gained this prominence, he learned that it derived from a test of strength. Years before, upon joining the group, Doc challenged the former leader to a fistfight. It was winning this contest that vaulted him into the leadership position and ejected the former leader from the gang.

His victory had given Doc a reputation for superior strength. Thereafter few wished to challenge him. But this reputation did more. It also provided him with a halo effect. Because he was physically superior, it was assumed that he was superior in other respects as well. For instance, it was believed that his ideas were better than those of his subordinates. When there was a question about what the group should do, his suggestions commanded the greatest deference. It was also assumed that he was a superior athlete. Thus when the group went bowling, Doc usually won.

One of the members of the gang, Frank, was, in fact, a gifted athlete. Frank was so well coordinated that he had won a tryout for the Boston Red Sox. And he was so physically dexterous that when Doc was absent, he was usually the best bowler. This led to teasing jousts when the both of them were on the way to the bowling alley. Frank would boastfully threaten to beat Doc, whereas Doc simply exhibited a quiet confidence. Then when the game was on the line, Frank invariably choked up. He was intimidated by Doc and never played up to his potential. Doc's reputation for strength, amplified his advantage.

Another member of the gang was even more anxious to displace Doc. His name was Chick and he was smart enough to know that he could not oust Doc in a direct confrontation. After many abortive attempts to persuade the group members to support him rather than Doc, Chick chose another path. He elected to go to college, where he ultimately earned an engineering degree. In essence, Chick took advantage of his superior intelligence to opt out of the street-corner-gang hierarchy and to seek elevation in a different ranking system. In time, he got a respectable job as an engineer, one that was occupationally superior to anything Doc could manage. It seems that we human beings do not have just one type of hierarchy in which to participate. Different sorts of activity require different sorts of strengths; therefore, the tests of strength required to move up within them differ. This enables people who cannot succeed in one ranking structure to succeed in another.

THE AMERICAN CLASS SYSTEM

The street corner gang was a circumscribed hierarchy. It involved a small number of players who obtained status in a limited field of supremacy. But there is a much more expansive hierarchy in which most of us participate. This is the social class system. Large-scale commercial societies distribute relative power largely, but not exclusively, in terms of economic dominance. They do not exhibit the precise sort of ranking found in face-to-face hierarchies, but a generalized sort of status that is correlated with wealth, yet involves other aspects of strength as well. Many people believe that class-based status is merely a matter of money; nevertheless, it has more to do with lifestyles than with raw affluence.

Let us begin with an overview of the American class system. We will divide it up into six classes, but before we do so, it must be emphasized that this is an arbitrary exercise. The social classes actually meld into each other in a seamless continuum. Naming them and distinguishing between them is merely a means of highlighting differences that might otherwise be less perceptible. This said, the upper-most class may be designated the upper-upper. It is not necessarily the segment of society with the most money, but that which has had these resources the longest. It is, in other words, "old money." It consists of the Rockefellers, the DuPonts, the

Kennedys, the Bushes, and so forth. Having inherited their wealth, they are comfortable with it and with the social leadership that has historically attached to their dynasties.

Next in line comes the lower-upper class. These folks are the "new money." From the point of view of their betters, they are *nouveau riche*. Perhaps very wealthy, they are nevertheless regarded as crass by those above them. People like Bill Gates and Ted Turner fit into this category. They may be worth billions of dollars and command powerful corporations, but they do not command the prerogatives of tradition. Turner, for instance, may be respected for his innovations in cable TV (i.e., CNN), but he is also dismissed as the "mouth of the South." Some of these lower-uppers are very powerful indeed. They are the CEOs of large organizations and the moving forces behind large-scale commercial and political ventures.

All told, the upper-upper class constitute about .5 percent of the population, while the lower-upper class represents about 2 percent. They are therefore only a small slice of the social pie. The upper-middle class represents a much larger segment, perhaps 40 percent. These people are the professionals, middle managers, and successful entrepreneurs of society. They are the community's professional planners, organizers, and risk takers. Doctors and lawyers, as well as college professors, engineers, and architects, inhabit this layer. Individually they may not be as powerful as members of the upper classes, but in a techno-commercial civilization such as ours they set the tone for much of what is done. Well educated and physically comfortable, they are accustomed to leadership positions.

Next down the social ladder comes the lower middle class. Many Americans prefer to think of themselves as in the middle of the middle, and perhaps they are, but for our purposes we will leave this level out. Lower-middles are primarily skilled workers. They may work in factories, in which case they operate complex machinery that takes expertise to manage. But they may also be craftspeople. They might be carpenters, electricians, plumbers, or machinists. They might also be police officers, firefighters, or long-distance truck drivers. Likewise in this category are social workers, elementary school teachers, nurses, and skilled secretaries. Like the upper-middles, these people are usually competent at what they do and are proud of their accomplishments. They also lead comfortable lives, and are frequently more affluent than those above them on the social scale.

Below the lower-middles comes the upper lower class. Together these two strata constitute the working class. They are typified by jobs that entail the use of one's hands. Unlike those above them who specialize in working with people or data, these individuals specialize in manipulating things. The difference between the upper-lowers and those who rank higher is that they are less accomplished. Their skills are not as great and do not take as much time or effort to acquire. If they work in factories, these people tend to be machine operators. If they work in construction, they tend to wield shovels or pick axes. Many work in less fancy restaurants as waiters and waitresses. Frequently hard working, their incomes are distinctly lower than those of their betters. Because they are by and large, less well educated than those above them, they are also less powerful.

Finally come the lower-lowers. These are the people at the bottom of the social hierarchy. Some of them are so low they belong to the underclass. These latter folks have been receiving public assistance intergenerationally and show little evidence of moving up. Some of the lower-lowers are also itinerant workers who, because they are chemically addicted, cannot hold down a steady job. In general, members of this stratum are the poorest paid members of the community doing the least skilled and dirtiest jobs. For the most part, they feel like failures and are regarded as such by others. And yet most lower-lowers who are physically and mentally able to do move up. Even most of those who begin their journey as hamburger flippers will progress. According to the government poverty level, those below this line constitute only about 12 percent of the population. There was a time when the social class hierarchy looked like a pyramid, with most people clustered at the base. Today, however, it is more like a diamond, with most hovering in the middle.

Still, one more distinction is essential. Many people confuse celebrity status with social status. They believe that if someone's face is plastered all over the media and/or if this person has earned a great deal of money, he or she must be upper class. They imagine that movie and rock stars along with athletes, because they are famous, are also socially powerful. In truth, individuals such as Anna Nicole Smith or Mike Tyson are merely well-known people with large bank accounts. They began in the lower class and many remain so despite their prominence. A look at their lifestyles, which in the case of Smith and Tyson have been tawdry in the extreme, should suffice to demonstrate that they never traveled above their roots. One was essentially always a stripper and the other a street thug, not above biting an opponent's ear off.

Social mobility, that is, moving from one social class into another, is far more difficult than most people imagine. Because it involves more than money, a person can become financially lucky without moving up the scale. In most cases, people travel no more than one notch in their lifetimes. There is also a tendency toward homogamy. Although there are many stories about people marrying into wealth, it is usually more comfortable for someone to form a close relationship with a person like himself or herself. Some, such as Anna Nicole, marry above themselves, but they never learn to comport themselves above their starting place. Others, like Cary Grant (who wed Woolworth heiress Barbara Hutton) marry into money, but become so uncomfortable they feel compelled to divorce.

MEASURING SOCIAL CLASS

So far we have taken an impressionistic tour of the class system. Now we must be a bit more scientific. Sociologists have not come up with a foolproof way of measuring relative status, but they do possess a good approximation. It is called socioeconomic status, or SES for short. An index composed of three indicators, this guideline attaches numbers to lifestyles. The first of these indicators is income. How much a person earns in dollars per year is simple to measure. It is not, however, as valid a gauge of status as is wealth. The problem is that the latter is notoriously difficult to pin down. A person may own huge swaths of land, yet how does one put a dollar figure to these acres before they are sold? The same applies to people whose wealth is denominated in art. What is an old master worth before it is placed on the market? This means that someone with old money might register lower on SES than her salaried employees. Even someone like Bill Gates would do poorly because Microsoft pays him a miniscule salary. His money derives from the stock ownership.

The second indicator of SES is education. This too is simple to measure in years of schooling. The problem here is that many people in the highest classes do not get much education. Already well situated economically, they do not need an advanced degree in order to get ahead. Even as undergraduates George W. Bush and John Kerry were prepared to settle for a gentlemen's C. It is not that they were less intelligent, but less motivated.

The final indicator of class is occupational prestige. It might be assumed that prestige being intangible, this would be difficult to determine. In fact, sociologists have been able to overcome this hurdle. Each year they send out survey instruments that ask a random sample of individuals to rank a variety of occupations according to their relative status. Surprisingly, these rankings turn out to be extremely consistent. Physicians always wind up near the top, while bootblacks and trash collectors cluster toward the bottom. In general, the dirtiest and most physical jobs are rated low on prestige, whereas those entailing the most social power and/or cerebral expertise are rated highest. Trash collectors make good money, but few admire the filth they must sort through. At the other end of the spectrum, Supreme Court justices are admired for their social importance, as well as their intellectual vigor.

Putting together these indicators yields some surprises. One reason why celebrities do so poorly is that although their incomes are high, their education and occupational prestige tend to be low. Sometimes people forget that a century ago entertainers were considered little better than prostitutes. On the opposite side of the hierarchical range, college professors rank higher than their incomes would seem to merit. This is because they score well on education and occupational prestige. They may not be able to afford splashy mansions, but their stature is such that people respect their opinions more than those of laypersons. As a result, they count as upper middle class even though they earn less than some assembly line workers.

SELF-DIRECTION VERSUS CONFORMITY

Melvin Kohn organized one of the most illuminating programs of research ever done about social class. He decisively demonstrated that one of the more enduring narratives about social class is a myth. Members of the middle class have routinely been castigated as conformists. They have been described as shallow followers who reflexively do the bidding of their upper-class masters. Once fabled as "men in gray flannel suits," they are said to be bland traditionalists who have a difficult time coming to conclusions for themselves. What Kohn discovered was that the opposite is true—that part of being middle class is being an independent thinker.

Kohn began with a research idea that at first might seem unrelated to his eventual findings. He started by inquiring into what sorts of values parents hold for their children. Initially in the United States, but eventually internationally, he asked members of various social strata what qualities they most appreciated in their offspring. To his surprise, he found consistent differences. Members of the upper middle class tended to endorse consideration of others, an interest in how and why things work, and personal responsibility. Those in the working classes tended to favor obedience and being neat and clean. Kohn wound up summarizing these tendencies by declaring that middle-class parents value self-direction, whereas working-class parents prefer conformity.

But Kohn did not stop here. He also asked the next logical question, namely: Why do middle-class parents treasure self-direction, while working-class parents choose conformity? This led him back to the sorts of occupations these adults hold. The upper-middle-class parents, Kohn realized, perform jobs that rely on self-direction. As professionals and middle managers, they are frequently called upon to make independent decisions, often in an environment of uncertainty. If they could not autonomously figure out how things worked, they might make unfortunate choices. Lawyers, to cite one sort of position, have to be able to think on their feet. When in a courtroom, they are not able to rely on directions from a boss, but need to be self-reliant experts. Moreover, because middle-class persons frequently operate in supervisory capacities they have to be both personally responsible and considerate of those they supervise. They need to be internally motivated to do their jobs well, while simultaneously being sensitive to the motivations of those they manage.

For working-class parents, their vocational environment is quite different. If they work in factories, for instance, they do not get to set their own schedules. These are dictated by their bosses, or sometimes by the machines they run. Their supervisors set production quotas at so many of this sort of widget and/or the assembly line chugs along at a predetermined pace. No matter how experienced the individual worker, he or she is expected to conform to externally established parameters. Sometimes this means that a worker with decades of practical knowledge has to take orders from a novice engineer fresh out of a technical college. These subordinate employees may hate to conform, but they have few alternatives.

Now, said Kohn, imagine what happens when these people get home. The middle-class professional is probably feeling pretty good about himself or herself at the end of the day. These persons have power on the job and this usually extends into their image of themselves. Consequently, when such a father gets home and his daughter asks him why the sky is blue, he patiently answers her question. He explains about the wavelengths of light and their diffraction in the upper atmosphere, and so forth. Although each answer elicits a fresh "Why" question, he remains serene because he wants her to understand and he appreciates her curiosity. Indeed, he wishes to encourage this independence of mind because he realizes it will place her in good stead when someday she enters a professionalized job.

The working-class father, however, is liable to exhibit a different attitude. After having been pushed around all day at work, he is in no mood to be pushed around at home—especially by his own child. Even though he hates conformity, he demands it of his daughter rather than to knuckle under to another external directive. Should she ask him why the sky is blue, the response will frequently be either, "Don't ask stupid questions" or "Go ask your mother." Patience will be in short supply as he seeks to decompress from occupational pressures. The consequence is nevertheless to discourage independent thought. The effect—albeit unconsciously—is to prepare his daughter for a world in which others set the standards. In this case, obedience, not personal responsibility, autonomous expertise, or interpersonal sensitivity is at a premium. Even cleanliness will matter to a parent who works at a dirty job.

This said, we can now explain the mystery with which the previous chapter ended: Why have methods of socialization changed so dramatically during the past several centuries? Why has corporal punishment gone out of style, as have swaddling clothes and wet nurses? And why has formal education expanded so greatly, to the point of creating a teenage culture? The answer is provided by the growing dominance of the middle classes. As more and more jobs become professionalized, that is, as more of them require self-motivated expertise, socialization techniques have been modified to produce what is in demand.

Clearly, with a greater need for technical proficiency has come a greater call for the sort of formal training that produces this expertise. Perhaps less obvious is the value placed on internalized motivation. The old style of discipline depended upon imposing external constraints. It demanded obedience from children who would grow up to perform roles that required compliance. Youngsters were literally frightened into submission. Today the idea is to help the young understand why they should behave one way rather than another. The goal is for them to make the appropriate choices without being told to do so by an external authority. This is why time-outs have become fashionable. The mischievous child who is sent to his room for having hit his little sister is not just being punished, he is also being asked to think about what he did and not come out until he recognizes why it was wrong. He is supposed to internalize this lesson so that he can later apply it on his own.

Something similar applies to swaddling. Swaddling prevented children from moving around. This interfered with their exploring their environment. In short, it discouraged curiosity. But curiosity is now wanted. Nowadays we go out of our way to provide infants with simulating toys that spark their imaginations. We also encourage mothers to raise their own children because we have learned that stable attachments in infancy lead to self-confidence in adulthood. Parents who wish their children to have the courage to make independent decisions in their later professional life seek to instill emotional security early on. They also seek to impose discipline in a way that it promotes self-control rather than a dependence on outer controls.

All in all, social mobility in a techno-commercial world derives from self-direction as opposed to conformity. But this can be difficult to achieve for those who have come to maturity in a working-class environment. Having grown up believing they are supposed to be obedient, they feel guilty exercising personal initiative. Thus, one of the functions of a college education is to encourage self-direction. The current educational buzzword "critical thinking" is really about self-direction. It is about being able to evaluate information independently and then courageously come to a personal conclusion. The technical knowledge that a higher education provides is not irrelevant, but it is less critical than an ability to seek out data as it is needed and to appraise its merit without having to rely on outside authorities.

SOCIAL CLASS LIFESTYLES

Earlier it was asserted that social class is more about lifestyles than income per se. This is because the lifestyles people select are connected with how they exercise social power. The ways that individuals enjoy themselves, how well they take care of their health, the manner in which they interact with others, and their organizational associations are all bound up with the degree to which they are self-directed. The more control they feel over their lives—the more they are, what psychologists would call, their own locus of control—the more they are likely to engage in activities over which they experience personal command.

This begins with the way they have fun. Upper-middle-class types are more likely to favor golf, whereas working-class folks prefer bowling. Although Mark Twain referred to golf as a good walk ruined, the infuriating niceties of the game are part of its attraction for independent decision makers. Not only do its foursomes allow people to talk business as they move from hole to hole, but the precision required to strike the ball well demands iron self-control. Bowling, in contrast, is a much quicker sport. The frames succeed each other with such rapidity that there is little waiting time. Then too there is the pleasing muscularity of knocking the pins down. While personal control is important, it is less demanding than in golf.

Middle-class types are also more apt to turn to reading for entertainment. They will pick up a book to get lost in its story or to expand their knowledge. Working class types are more apt to regard reading as an onerous chore. Unlikely to get beyond the sports pages of the newspaper, they look upon reading as an academic exercise in which one engages only when it is required. They are more likely to engage in physical pastimes. Weekends are more apt to find them tinkering with their automobiles than going to the ballet.

Members of the middle-class are also more liable to plan ahead. Since this is what they do at work, they bring the habit home. These people are list makers; they are routine keepers. The are also comfortable postponing gratifications; that is, if they believe they can obtain more by consuming resources tomorrow rather than today, tomorrow it will be. Working-class persons are more spontaneous. When opportunities arise, they are more apt to leap at them. Thus if a friend offers them a beer, they are likely to sit down and join the festivities, whereas middle-class individuals are inclined to beg off so as to keep appointments they previously contracted.

These tendencies have consequences for the health of those involved. Upper-middle-class types have better health. In thinking ahead, they consider the long-term implications of their choices. Thus, if drinking too much alcohol is bad for the liver, this is sufficient reason to abstain. For working-class individuals, on the other hand, beer may be regarded as a funda-mental food type, with anything less than a six-pack dismissed as going dry. No wonder that jogging and salad for lunch have been middle-class innovations. For the working-class, steak and potatoes remains the ideal.

Some people believe that those high on the social class ladder have better health because they can afford better medical care. There is some truth to this, but it is overshadowed by dif-ferences in how the classes utilize medical facilities. In fact, most working-class people have medical insurance, while Medicaid covers those in poverty. A more significant disparity lies in how they relate to medical practitioners. For those in the middle class physicians are their peers. They are therefore at ease relating their symptoms to them, which is the single best tech-nique for obtaining an accurate diagnosis. They are also apt to follow the doctor's recommen-dations. For those in the working class, the doctor is someone of higher status. This, unfortu-nately, creates resentments. To his or her face the physician receives deference, but outside the consulting room there is oppositionalism. At this point, the doctor may be disparaged as a tin god and his or her prescriptions ignored. The result is that the lower the social class, the worse the health.

Out in the political sphere, preexisting differences in social power are exacerbated by atti-tudes toward organizational participation. Middle-class types are much more likely to be join-ers. They are not intimidated by groups of strangers and are more apt to articulate their opin-ions. Working-class individuals are more inclined to shy away. They fatalistically believe that "you can't fight city hall," so they never try. Less disposed to vote, they are also less disposed to become members of political action committees or professional organizations. And if they do join these associations, they are not likely to enter their leadership. Those in the middle class are much more cognizant of the value of networking. They understand that if you put out feelers, you may make connections with others who will someday prove helpful.

Moreover, because they are less confident in their abilities, those lower in the social scale are apt to be louder and splashier in how they relate to each other. Instead of modesty and understated elegance, they opt for boastfulness and overstatement. Fearful of being overlooked, they seek to stand out from the crowd. Like the wrestlers they so much admire, they may be in-your-face brash and coercive. Unfortunately, this generally has the opposite effect from that desired. Instead of projecting strength, it projects weakness. Instead of garnering social assis-tance, it provokes opposition. A much better strategy would be political horse-trading, but this takes a willingness to give as well as receive. It presupposes the personal confidence that is typ-ically foreign to those who have been oppressed by a need to be obedient to others.

Another part of the lifestyle of the upper middle class, but not of the lower-classes, is introspection. Generally the best starting point in understanding others, and therefore for leading them, is self-understanding. One needs the courage to examine both one's strengths and weaknesses. A realistic appreciation of this is enormously helpful in deciding where best to apply one's energies. It is also enormously useful in perceiving the fears and desires of others, which in turn facilitates interacting with them in ways that are influential.

Last, family relationships vary by class. The home has been likened to a haven in a heartless world. For members of the middle class this refuge—this place where one can go to recharge one's emotional batteries—is provided by a companionate marriage. Husbands and wives who feel like moral equals and collaborate in solving mutual problems give each other the strength to persevere. Members of the working and lower classes, however, are more likely to exhibit skewed marriages. These husbands and wives fight over power to such an extent that they may prefer to pursue many of their activities separately. He trundles off to the neighborhood bar to lift a few with the boys, while she gets on the phone to commiserate with her mother. Unfortunately, this is not a prescription for greater success.

Collectively, this means that as people move up the social scale they must change the way they behave. If they are to relate to others in a more self-directed way, they have to become people who are more capable of self-direction. They need to develop the personal controls and interpersonal skills required of self-motivated experts who are capable of providing competent leadership for others. Yet this is not easy. Education helps, but emotional and personal growth are also essential. How one deals with others, and not just a craving for power or a large income, is crucial to developing the interpersonal alliances that are indispensable in winning tests of strength in market-oriented, techno-commercial societies.

Questions

1. How do you feel about losing? How do you react to winning? Do you know any contented losers?
2. To which social class do you belong? What class would you prefer to be a part of?
3. Have you been able to engage in social mobility? What difficulties have you encountered?
4. What sort of social class socialization did you undergo? Did it prepare you for self-direction or conformity?

Selected Readings

de Waal, F. 1982. *Chimpanzee Politics*. New York: Harper & Row.

Fussell, P. 1983. *Class: A Guide through the American Status System*. New York: Simon & Schuster.

Kohn, M. L. 1969. *Class and Conformity: A Study in Values*. Homewood, IL.: The Dorsey Press.

Wolfe, A. 1996. *Marginalized in the Middle*. Chicago: University of Chicago Press.

A Tribal Imperative?: Race and Ethnicity

RACISM

It is no secret that racism has been prevalent in the United States. The country has a long history of treating African Americans as second-class persons. It has ranked them below others and regarded them as individually inferior. Despite a Declaration of Independence that asserts all men (and women) are created equal, for over two centuries this judgment did not apply to blacks. Like social class, the resulting disparity is an instance of social stratification. It is a case in point in which one's hierarchical position is based on race—a circumstance where some are treated worse than others on account of their biological heritage.

But racism does not operate like social class. It has more in common with a caste system than a class system. In the case of class, social mobility is possible. If a person earns more money and/or acquires more power, he or she can rise in the rankings. In a caste system, this is not possible. Theoretically, at least, there is no social mobility. The social station into which one is born is the one he or she will retain for the rest of his or her life. In this kind of system, should a person attempt to rise above her- or himself, he or she will be severely sanctioned. He or she may even be put to death.

The classic illustration of a caste system is found in India. In the Hindu system there are four primary castes. On the top are the Brahmins. They are the priestly order and are regarded as sacred. Next come the Kshatriyas. These are the warriors. Below them come the Vaisyas. They are the merchants. On the bottom are the Sudras, that is, the peasants. And at the very bottom of the Sudras are the Untouchables. So unclean are they supposed to be that that those above them are literally not allowed to touch them. For their part, when they encounter individual Brahmins, they are supposed to take off their shoes and walk past them silently. Should a Sudra man decide to marry a Brahmin woman, the results historically were liable to be fatal for both. Moving out of one's caste was simply not permitted.

All of this is supported by a religious ideology. The Hindu religion preaches transmigration of souls. When an individual dies, his or her soul is thought to travel into another body, where it is reborn. What sort of physical vessel this will be depends upon the moral character of the soul. During one's lifetime one builds up a supply of Karma. The greater the fund of Karma, the higher the level of organism into which one will be reborn. A very good Sudra, for instance, might be reincarnated as a Brahmin, whereas a very bad Brahmin could return as a Sudra. A truly evil person might even come back as a cockroach. What you are in any particular life is therefore a matter of your spiritual worth and can no more be changed than a donkey can become a king.

Among American blacks the situation has not been all that different. They were formerly held down by a slave system, as opposed to a caste system. Yet the consequences were similar. They too were believed to be organically inferior and held in their place by a religious mandate. According to many white Southerners, the Bible decreed that the offspring of Ham were to be hewers of wood and drawers of water. Cursed because their remote ancestor defied the word of God, they were condemned to become eternal children. Less intelligent than others, they needed to be ruled over by their betters. Only in this way could they be civilized and Christianized.

Given this mentality, should a black man have sex with a white woman, the sentence was death, often by lynching. Should a black man even look at a white woman lasciviously, a lynching might result. No matter how successful a black became, he or she was still regarded as inferior. Should a white and black meet on the sidewalk, it was the black who was expected to step aside. This sort of deference was demanded not only during slavery, but in the Jim Crow era that followed the Civil War. The idea that an African American could rise to be president of the country or CEO of a major corporation was laughable. Nothing could remove the stigma of being black or induce a white to submit to the descendent of a slave.

This sort of rigid hierarchical imperative developed out of historical tests of strength where one community decisively defeated another. In India this occurred when the invading pastoral Aryans asserted their supremacy over the indigenous agricultural Dravidians. In this case, the Aryans demanded that the darker-skinned locals accede to the Aryan religion, while they simultaneously kept working the land. The reason that blacks became inferior to whites in America is that when Europeans first ventured down the coast of Africa, they possessed a decisive military advantage. Their ships were much larger than those of the indigenous peoples, but more important, these craft carried cannons on their decks. This provided the Europeans the firepower to enslave the Africans, and, after the discovery of America, to employ them for profit on sugar, and later tobacco and cotton, plantations. This is what disenfranchised dark-skinned Africans and kept them suppressed for centuries. This is what created their reputation for inferiority and fueled the racist sentiments of their masters.

Some have sought to evade this hierarchical trap by claiming there is only one race, namely, the human race. But were this so, there could never have been anything called racism because racial distinctions would have been impossible. The question then arises as to how many races there are, and the answer in this case turns out to be arbitrary. There may be racial differences, but different populations blend into each other in such a manner that there are no hard and fast lines. If one travels to Uzbekistan, for instance, one may be hard pressed to determine whether the inhabitants are Caucasian or Mongoloid. Similar issues arise in Egypt concerning whether ordinary people are Caucasian or Negroid. In fact, where one draws the boundaries between groups is a political decision. Those who assert there are no races are fond of pointing out that these definitions about race are not scientific—and they are not. But that does not make them less real. It only makes them inexact and unofficial.

Most people can tell the difference between people whose ancestors hail from Sweden and those whose roots are in Nigeria. There exist visual distinctions that we human beings are prepared to notice. But these perceptible differences may not be the best guide as to how closely various populations are related. Fortunately, nowadays we possess a tool that enables us to make these judgments. Genetic researchers have developed techniques for determining biological relatedness. On this basis it has become conventional to identify four primary races: the Caucasoid, Mongoloid, Negroid, and Australoid. The last refers to the indigenous inhabitants of Australia and New Guinea. On the surface they look like Negroids, that is, they have dark skin, broad noses, and kinky hair. But appearances are deceptive. An examination of their DNA demonstrates that they are among the least closely related to the Negroids.

The lesson is that race is real, but not clear cut. There are inherited biological differences between various groups, yet these are not precise. Nor are they free of bias. The people who constitute the majority of contemporary Mexicans thus exhibit a combination of Caucasoid and Mongoloid traits. They are the successors of Native Americans and invading Spanish conquistadors. But does this mean they are inferior? Some upper-class Mexicans seem to think so, but the so-called mestizos refer to themselves as La Raza and believe that their combined ancestry makes them superior to others. The French have an adage that is appropriate to this situation. They say, at nights all cats are black. Racism may be part of the human heritage, but so is crossing racial boundaries. Virtually wherever people have traveled, they have left genetic deposits behind them. As a consequence, it is foolish to speak of racial purity or to make judgments about others based upon this fabled inviolability.

RACIAL DIFFERENCES

When discussing race, the most important thing to understand is how closely all human beings are related to all other human beings. There may be a multitude of differences, but these tend to be trivial and superficial. Let us begin at the beginning. We human beings all belong to the same species. We are all Homo Sapiens. A species consists of a group of individuals who produce fertile offspring when they mate. As it happens, members of any given human race can mate with members of any other race and create children who are themselves capable of having children. As a species, we seem to go back about one hundred and fifty thousand years. All of our ancestors, no matter what their color or physiognomy, can trace their lineage to East Africa. It is there that we find the earliest evidence of our forefathers and foremothers.

There is, however, a defining moment in our past that underlines how closely we are related. Approximately seventy-five thousand years ago an incident occurred that almost wiped out our species. The Toba caldera located in central Sumatra spectacularly exploded. In doing so, it sent up clouds of ash so vast that they generated a worldwide "nuclear winter." Sunlight could not penetrate to the surface; hence plants died, as did the animals that fed off these plants and the animals that fed off the herbivores. This included our ancestors. It is estimated that the total human population declined to about seventy thousand individuals. It was only after this genetic bottleneck that people began to migrate out of Africa in serious numbers.

Genetic indicators have become so sophisticated that is it now possible to trace the broad outlines of this migration. We have learned, for instance, that the reason that Australoids and Negroids are so distantly related is that the predecessors of today's indigenous Australians were among the first to split off from the African rootstock. They were able to travel by foot along the northern border of the Indian Ocean when sea levels were much lower than today, thanks to the concurrent Ice Age. We now also understand that the Caucasians who came to inhabit Europe first settled in central Asia before venturing west. They could not make it to their eventual homeland before the continental ice sheets melted away.

What interests most of us, however, is how the visible differences between the races arose. These, we now realize, are owed to a phenomenon known as *genetic drift*. It seems that mutations are always occurring among human beings. Most of these are trivial and unhelpful, but some have functional implications. In any event, as long as populations remain in contact, they can exchange genetic materials. When, however, they are separated, the newly evolved genes of one group do not have an opportunity to suffuse through the other. They therefore develop distinctive characteristics. This is what occurred as glaciers, mountains, and/or deserts interceded between formerly homogenous populations.

It is estimated that it would take about twenty thousand years for a dark-skinned people to become a light-skinned population through the agency of genetic drift. In this instance the change would stick if in the intervening years they migrated from a southern to a northern latitude. Since there is less sunlight in the north, they would benefit from a reduction in melanin. This would permit more sun to penetrate their skin to produce the vitamin D that their metabolisms require. Although most genetic drift would result in arbitrary modifications, some would introduce clearly beneficial variations. These would, needless to say, survive a winnowing-out process.

In any event, a multitude of local adaptations ultimately produced the plethora of differences today on display. The "one race" advocates may wish to deny these deviations, but they exist. Although they are not neatly packaged in consistent racial subdivisions, they are plainly discernable. Let us commence with some obvious ones. Many people say race is about skin color, and this is part of what is involved—yet only part. Color is noticeable, but it is also capriciously distributed. Thus, Sudanese Arabs who insist on their Caucasian connections are nearly as dark skinned as the Negroid peoples they oppress. Hair texture is also very noticeable. African Americans frequently distinguish between good and bad skin, and good and bad hair. In the latter case, they differentiate between straight and kinky hair. Tightly curled shafts tend to be associated with an equatorial residence because it provides better protection against direct sunlight. Even though it may seem to indicate a substantial genetic difference, it results from hair that is elliptical rather than round in cross-section. Incidentally, Mongoloid peoples tend to have the roundest cross-sections and therefore the straightest hair.

There are also differences in hair color, eye color, eye shape, length of nose, broadness of nose, fullness of lips, height of cheekbones, and distinctness of chin. Some of these seem to have functional repercussions, whereas others are apparently arbitrary. Length of nose, for instance, is associated with dry climates. A longer proboscis evidently allows more space to introduce humidity to air that is breathed in, which is better for the lungs. What service full lips might provide is another matter entirely. These may have esthetic functions, but if they furnish some other service, this remains undeciphered. Two more variations that should be mentioned are facial prognathism and head shape. Prognathism refers to the angle an imaginary line from the bridge of the nose to the upper lip makes with the rest of the face. This incline tends to be largest among Negroids and least among Mongoloids. Meanwhile, some groups have long heads and some wide heads; they are dolichocephalic and brachycephalic, respectively. Here it is Caucasians who are most dolichocephalic and Mongoloids who are most brachycephalic.

Now we come to something that is more controversial—something that got sportscaster Jimmy the Greek fired from network television. Many people have observed that there are differences in body types and that some of these are related to athletic abilities. Some of these allegations are flat-out false. Negroids do not possess bones that other races do not. Yet there is some truth to assertions regarding a supposed "white man's disease." In basketball it is said that white men can't jump; and, in fact, blacks do tend to jump higher than whites. This seems to be associated with variations in muscle composition. There are two types of voluntary muscles: fast twitch and slow twitch. Negroids whose ancestry traces to West (but not East) Africa have a larger proportion of fast-twitch muscles. These are best suited to quick movements such at those necessary for jumping or finishing first in short dashes. Slow-twitch muscles are more suited to activities that require endurance, such as marathons. It is necessary to recognize that these race-related differences are very small, but can sometimes spell victory or failure in athletic contests.

Even more awkward, but for that very reason something that should be dealt with openly, is the issue of what some people refer to as "booty." Booty has become a big issue within the African American community because there is a difference in the size of buttocks between whites and blacks. Blacks tend to have larger derrieres. But, remarkably enough, there is an explanation for this. It is associated with climate rather than sunlight. People in cold climates need more body insulation than those in warm ones. Evolution has arranged for this by distributing body fat more evenly among Caucasians than Negroids. In Negroids, where fat cells need to be out of the way to facilitate cooling, they are concentrated in the rump.

There are other, less visible disparities between the races. Mongoloids, for instance, tend to be more lactose intolerant that Northern Europeans. This is why you have never heard of Chinese cheesecake. Negroids also tend to have more sickle cell anemia. This is because the sickle cell trait provides protection against the malaria that is omnipresent in sub-Sahara Africa. But because this disease is also prevalent in the Mediterranean basin, many of its residents also suffer from sickle cell anemia, even though they are Caucasian.

Finally, there is the issue that most exercises racists. Intelligence, too, is not particularly visible. Yet it is of such importance that its absence is equated with inferiority. Certainly Negroids have been accused of being less intelligent than other groups. Stephan Jay Gould, to cite one example, discusses the mistaken nineteenth-century notion that blacks have smaller brains than whites in his book *The Mismeasure of Man*. He also demonstrates that this conclusion followed from the prejudices of that era. In fact, there is no conclusive evidence of racial differences in IQ. People of every race exhibit comparable mental abilities.

Yes, there are race-based differences, but these are merely differences. They are not, on this account, inherently better or worse. Assertions that they are, are moral judgments; they are not scientific observations. No human population is intrinsically morally superior to any other. Despite their differences, it must always be remembered that people are, first and foremost, human.

ETHNIC DIFFERENCES

The same sorts of questions can be asked about ethnicity that have been asked about race. To begin with, how many different ethnic groups are there? And are these differences biological in origin? Many people assume that ethnic groupings are like large families. They imagine that they can trace their beginnings to a single legendary ancestor. But this seems to be more myth than reality. Ethnic distinctions, as opposed to racial ones, concentrate more on cultural rather than biological distinctions. This means that there are many more ethnic categories than racial ones and that these classifications are more mutable.

Some years ago a college student took a trip to Europe. Before he disembarked on the ferry from England to Belgium, he took the time to brush up on his high school French. As he did not want to be perceived as an ugly American, he was determined to speak to the locals in their own language. Thus when he landed in Ostende, he asked in French for directions to the nearest youth hostel. Much to his surprise, he was greeted with hostility. The people he asked turned away in a huff. At first he thought they were offended by his American accent, but when he gave up and asked for help in English, the response was utterly different. Now the people he approached not only answered, they even escorted him to where he was going.

What the young man did not understand was that Ostende is located in the Flemish-speaking part of Belgium. Its residents not only don't speak French, they are antagonistic toward the Walloons who do. If asked about their ethnic identity, members of these factions would not reply that they are Belgian, but that they are Flemish or Walloon, respectively. How, then, did the two come to reside in a single nation? The answer is that their country came into existence after the Napoleonic wars. It was carved out of what had been the Greater Netherlands because the Flemings and Walloons, both of whom were Catholic, objected to being included in a Protestant nation.

The Greater Netherlands, in its turn, had once been incorporated into a still larger nation. The Spanish once controlled the country. Almost a hundred years of war were required to assert independence. Indeed, when the king of Spain sent his Armada to conquer Elizabethan England, the plan was to stop off in the Netherlands to pick up the army then fighting to suppress Dutch nationalism.

The point of this digression is that ethnic identities are based on three primary factors: language, religion, and physical proximity. Peoples who speak the same tongue frequently imagine that they possess identical biological roots. Likewise, those who share a common religion may assume that they are part of a single spiritual family. Last, being in close proximity to others facilitates the interactions that provide a sense of similarity. Too much distance allows factionalism to develop, as well as resentments about being ruled by outsiders. This is a major reason why colonies, including the United States, frequently seek independence.

Given these determinants of ethnic identity, how peoples view themselves can change when these determining factors change. France is today thought of as a single nation inhabited primarily by a uniform French people, but this ignores how this uniformity was achieved. The people in the southwest once spoke a language called the langue d'oc. They became French in their identification only after they were conquered by northerners who spoke the langue d'oui, that is, by those from the isle de France for whom *oui* was the word for *yes*. Brittany in the northwest of the country became French in identity even more recently. Its inhabitants stubbornly considered themselves Bretons until their children were coerced into learning French in school.

Religious conversion also can alter ethnic connections. One of the more sanguine episodes in recent European history can be traced to this sort of event. When Yugoslavia fell apart, it descended into a three-way contest for political supremacy. The Croats hated the Serbs, who detested the Bosnians, who had not much use for the Croats. Their hostilities were so severe, even featuring ethnic cleansing, that one might imagine they were totally unrelated peoples. In fact, they speak what is essentially the same language, namely Serbo-Coatian. Oddly, their differences can be traced back to the Roman Empire. Not long before this domain disintegrated, its rulers tried to make it more manageable by dividing it into eastern and western segments, the one controlled from Constantinople and the other by Rome. The line between them fell roughly along the contemporary border between the Croats and Serbs.

What this resulted in was the separation of what had been a distinct people. One manifestation of this division was that the Croats adopted the Roman script, whereas the Serbs embraced a Greek-based script. Another expression of their partition was that the Croats became Roman Catholics, whereas the Serbs became Greek Orthodox. The Bosnians, however, came under a third influence. They straddled the border between the Croats and Serbs; hence when the Moslem Ottomans subsequently conquered their territory, they were susceptible to conversion. Offered the opportunity to embrace Islam in return for a reduction in taxes, they accepted this exchange.

Today these three populations stare at each other in mutual hatred despite their derivation from the same tribal stock. They seem to believe that what today distinguishes them is indelibly part of who they are. The truth, however, is that their current self-images grew out of specifiable historical events. Changes in their religious commitments, more than anything else, converted them into die-hard enemies.

Ethnicity is so malleable largely because where people live, the languages they speak, and the religions they espouse are so readily modified. Consider the derivation of several European place names. Find a map and inspect the northwest corner of Spain. It is called Galicia. This is because Gauls once inhabited it. The same Celtic people that Caesar conquered in France, the same ones who in Ireland speak Gaelic, were once also dominant in northern Iberia. Yet there is another Galicia. This one is in southern Poland. And—surprise, surprise—it is because the Celts once resided here as well. Those familiar with the New Testament will also realize that Paul wrote epistles to the Galatians. These too resided in an area once populated by Celts, but this region is located in central Turkey. The Celts undoubtedly moved around. But in this movement, they were not alone. Folk migrations are a common phenomenon. Yet when they occur, so do transformations in language, religion and spatial contiguity, and therefore ethnic identity.

As with race, once ethnic identities are established, members of different groups can deal with each other on the basis of something comparable to racism. Even though what separates them is not biological, one group can consider itself superior and then treat the other as inferior. Thus the Jews on the basis of their religion were considered less than human by the Nazis and subjected to genocide. Another ethnic group, the so-called Hispanics, are nowadays frequently regarded as second rate because of their language. Even within groups that are themselves the target of race-based intolerance, ethnic fanaticism can occur. This is currently the situation in Nigeria. There the hostilities between Yorubas and Ibos can reach a fevered pitch. Indeed, there was not so long ago a war between them. Even now the losers, that is, the Ibos,

often face discrimination if they enter Yoruba areas. With the Hausas, who are Moslems from the northern part of the country, similar tensions prevail.

PREJUDICE, DISCRIMINATION, AND STEREOTYPING

For many years, one of the most popular beers in New York City was Rheingold. And one of the company's more successful promotions was its annual contest to elect a Miss Rheingold. Pictures of the six contestants were prominently featured in the subway cars and ballots could be found in most grocery stores. Each year the winner was typically an attractive, blue-eyed blond. This was the case even though many New Yorkers had roots in Eastern and Southern Europe. Italians and Jews, in particular, tended toward dark hair and swarthy complexions. Nevertheless, they too voted for the blue-eyed blondes. Having been raised in America, this was their idea of beauty too.

It turns out that what people consider beautiful is related to social power. Because in the United States the most powerful ethnic groups have tended to derive from the original immigrant stock, peoples originating in Northwest Europe have set the standards for physical attractiveness. Because they tended to be fair, beauty came to be associated with being fair. Nevertheless, once upon a time, when the Romans dominated Europe, their tastes dictated standards of attractiveness. The Romans, for instance, greatly admired what they called the noble Roman nose. This was an aquiline nose. Aquiline means "like an eagle." In other words, the noble Roman nose was a large, hooked nose. Needless to say, with the emergence of Northern European dominance, their smaller, straighter noses became the standard.

When people think about prejudice, what comes to mind is usually negative prejudice. But prejudice can be both positive and negative. To be prejudiced is to prejudge. It is to have an attitude toward people based on their group membership, irrespective of their personal qualities. To be prejudiced often means considering individuals inferior simply because of their racial or ethnic identity. But it can also mean considering them special because of these identities. Discrimination, as opposed to prejudice, is about behavior. It is to treat people in a particular way because of their racial or ethnic identities. For the most part, we think of negative discrimination, such as refusing to hire someone because of the color of his or her skin, but there can also be positive discrimination, as in playing favorites with respect to women who are considered beautiful thanks to their communal affiliation.

Racism, which is a combination of prejudice and discrimination, may lead us to believe that the two always go together, but this need not be so. It is possible to be prejudiced without discriminating, and to discriminate without being prejudiced. One might, for example, hate African Americans, but upon entering the military discover that acting on this attitude would destroy one's career. Because the military frowns on bigotry, those who behave in this way, regardless of their personal feelings, find themselves subjected to institutional pressures to cooperate with all of their fellow soldiers. Overt discrimination can easily result in a demotion or a bad-conduct discharge, hence it is suppressed.

Stereotyping is another matter. Although it is often confused with prejudice and/or discrimination, it need not be associated with either. Nor does it, as some imagine, automatically produce racism or ethnic cleansing. Stereotyping is cognitive phenomenon. It is not about attitudes or behaviors, but beliefs. A stereotype is a simplified generalization about a group of people. As such, it may or may not be an accurate reflection of characteristics of this group.

Moreover, sometimes stereotypes are flattering. Beyond this, there are times they are passed down through the generations and times they are not.

Prejudice and discrimination tend to arise when groups compete for power. When one population becomes dominant over another, the losers are liable to be treated badly. In the case of Europeans versus Africans, the Africans were thrust into slavery. It is difficult to imagine a more virulent form of discrimination than this. But the winners also became prejudiced against blacks. They developed attitudes that justified treating these other human beings badly. If blacks were judged to be inherently inferior, then it made sense for their betters to order them around. This coercion would be for their own good. In time, this version of racism was passed down from one generation to the next via socialization. It became institutionalized and those inculcated in it came to regard it as a fact of nature.

Something comparable can happen between ethnic groups. When one population moves into the territory occupied by another, they may not meet as equals. Thus, when the Aryans conquered the Dravidians, they submerged the losers in a caste system. Conversely, when migrants from Eastern and Southern Europe arrived in the United States, they were considered inferior by those already established on the continent. Disembarking with little money, and speaking indecipherable tongues, the newcomers found niches at the bottom of the economic ladder. They became ditch-diggers or garment workers, and were regarded as deserving no better by those above them. Many of the natives even believed them to be inassimilable.

Stereotypes fit into this picture because they may be thought of as group reputations. When one population loses a contest to another, their relative weaknesses become salient. It is readily perceived that the losers dress differently, talk differently, and live differently, but these characteristics then become associated with their lower status and are believed to explain it. Why do Jews fail to get jobs in larger corporations?—Why, it is because they are clannish. And why are Italians treated with suspicion?—Well it is because so many of them are connected with the Mafia. Or what is the reason that blacks are confined to dirty jobs or to those in the entertainment industry?—Surely it is because they are less intelligent, less well educated, but perhaps have better rhythm than others. These reputations, which are based upon relative weakness, are then further generalized thanks to the halo effect. If members of a group exhibit difficulties in one area, they may be thought to have limitations in others as well. This then prompts others to treat them as if these limitations were inherent in their nature.

But stereotypes can be more benign. Most of us are aware of the stereotypes prevalent within our society, but we do not necessarily act upon them. Most of us, for instance, understand that Jews have a reputation for being smart, for making money, and for being good lawyers. Similarly, it is difficult to think about Italians without associating them with images derived from *The Sopranos* television show. By the same token, rednecks are thought illiterate and as fond of fast cars capable of outrunning the revenuers. Blacks of course, are associated with athletics and crime. We can be conscious of all of these generalizations, and even give them credence, without interacting with others based upon them. We may well treat individual Jews, Italians, rednecks, and blacks as distinctive persons, that is, as distinct from the stereotypes.

First, as psychologists have recently become aware, stereotyping is a normal mental mechanism. Just as we cannot prevent ourselves from indulging in some degree of ethnocentrism, so we cannot help generalizing about complex phenomena. Generalizations help us make sense of what might otherwise be too complicated to grasp. Indeed our ability to generalize has been an essential tool in coping with a multifaceted universe. It is this faculty that puts us a cut above horses and mountain lions. Because intergroup relations are complex, they too, of necessity, are shot through with stereotypes.

Second, stereotypes are functional in a *Gesellschaft* society. In a world in which most people are strangers to one another stereotypes act as calling cards. If you know nothing about an unfamiliar person except his or her ethnic identity, this stereotype gives you information that might come in handy. An illustration of this occurred when a teenage Danish visitor to the United States decided to visit Harlem. He had long heard about this place and, for him, it elicited romantic visions. A co-counselor at the camp where the two were employed, one who had experience working in Harlem, volunteered to provide a tour. Together they sauntered done 125th Street, one of the neighborhood's main arteries, with the Dane gawking as they went. Soon they spotted a group of young men loitering on a corner about a block ahead. These guys were chatting with each other and occasionally passing small packets between them. The Dane's eyes opened wide and he grabbed his camera to take a picture. At this point, his guide quickly demanded that he put it away. He, as opposed to his European visitor, was aware of American stereotypes. Even though he could not exactly see what was being exchanged, his stereotype led him to suspect that they were witnessing a series of drug deals. Someone without this generalized belief would not have arrived at this conclusion, with results that might have been unfortunate.

Third, stereotypes can be more or less accurate. To begin with stereotypes are usually grounded in realities. They may be simplified generalizations, but they typically derive from actual observations. Thus it is true that Jews as a group are the best-educated and financially most successful individuals in the United States. It is also true that a disproportionate number of them are lawyers. But it is not true that all, or even most Jews, are smart, rich, or attorneys. What is valid for the group may be far from valid for the individual. Likewise, the Mafia is, in fact, grounded in Italian culture. But most Italians are honest upstanding individuals who are not part of the syndicate. Nevertheless, they too know that the family loyalty emblematic of southern Italy is one of the reasons the mob has been so successful.

Fourth, the real difficulty with stereotypes occurs when people fail to particularize. If all one knows about a person is his or her group membership, one can be forgiven for initially assuming that he or she shares the alleged characteristics of the group. If, however, one gets to know that person, and has occasion to learn that the stereotype does not apply, yet one continues to apply it, this is evidence of bigotry. Colin Powell, former secretary of state, is famous for asserting that he does not have rhythm. Those who have heard him attempt to sing know this is true. But if someone were to insist that he must have rhythm because he is black, this would not only be wrong, but an indicator of prejudice. In a social-class-based society, where individual merit is supposed to lead to social mobility, it would deny a person recognition for his or her personal achievements.

Fifth, stereotypes can change. As facts on the ground are altered, so can stereotypes be altered. If stereotypes originally derive from reality, and if these realities, such as power relationships, are transformed, so may the generalizations based on them. Thus, there was a time when the Japanese were considered small and poor Asians who were only capable of copying the technological feats of others. This was because they were small, relatively poor, and did copy the achievements of Western societies. But this is no longer so. The Japanese are now better nourished and fairly wealthy. They have also become technological innovators. As such, they are far more widely respected than they once were. Similarly, African Americans were formerly considered too unintelligent to function as quarterbacks or coaches in professional football. But those days are gone forever. There have been many successful black quarterbacks and even a Super Bowl where both of the head coaches were black. Under these circumstances the old stereotype is no longer persuasive.

ASSIMILATION AND PLURALISM

At the beginning of the twentieth century it was normal to describe the United States as a melting pot. Conventional wisdom had it that divergent groups migrated to this country, whereupon they dissolved into the prevailing culture and became an integral constituent of the larger community. By the 1960s, however, this metaphor was rejected as hopelessly naïve. At this point, the metaphor was switched to that of a tossed salad. More highly educated Americans looked at their society and saw a bowl of mixed greens and vegetables that jostled side by side, but nonetheless maintained their separate identities. Different ethnic groups came to the country, then moved into neighborhoods peopled primarily by individuals from their former homelands. There thus arose a plethora of diverse Italian neighborhoods, Polish neighborhoods, and black neighborhoods, where people honored their traditional cultures while simultaneously affirming their American citizenship.

In the last couple of decades, another metaphor has emerged. This one alludes to a stew pot. A stew is composed of a number of different ingredients. Typically cubes of meat are coated in flour and then braised in the pot before vegetables such as potatoes, carrots, and peas are added, together with a liquid such as beef broth. All of these components are then simmered for several hours. Eventually there is a transformation. Some of the ingredients, such as the meat and carrots, maintain their integrity, whereas the potatoes gets soft around the edges and some of the peas explode, in both cases contributing to the sauce binding all into a single dish. In general, the longer the constituents cook, the more they lose their individuality and become part of the mush. Some, however, never do enter the whole. They continue to stand identifiably apart.

The American society is alleged to be like a stew pot in that the longer the ethnic groups have been present, the more likely they are to surrender their identity to a common American identification. This has been the case with the English, the Scotch-Irish, and the Germans. Many of the descendants of these groups are not even aware of their heritage. They surely do not live in English, Scotch-Irish, or German neighborhoods. Migrants with a shorter history in the United States, such as the Irish and the Italians, may or may not have assimilated into the whole. Some continue to reside in identifiable ethic enclaves, whereas others do not. It is the most recent migrants, such as Mexicans and Dominicans, who are the most likely to reside in ethnic communities. There is also the fact that some groups have resisted entering the mainstream. Religious denominations such as the Amish and Hutterites have insisted on remaining separate no matter how long their sojourn in this country.

A major distinction in terms of who assimilates and who does not pertains to the cultures that people bring with them when they migrate. Those whose cultures of origin are most compatible with the techno-commercial society they are entering have the least difficulty adjusting. Conversely, those with the largest differences experience the greatest struggles in blending in. Peasant populations, such as those from southern Italy, have taken longer to adjust than urban populations such as Eastern European Jews, even though the Jews were of a different religion than most Americans. The same considerations apply to Mexican migrants, who, like the Italians before them, tend to have peasant roots. Still, if history is a guide, they may take longer to fit in, but, in time, will do so.

The one major exception to this pattern is the situation of African Americans. As the only community with a history of having been slaves in the United States, they faced exclusionary pressures far greater than others did. Racism has kept them apart regardless of their personal proclivities. As the victims of a caste system, they were not allowed to live where they wished or to marry whomever they chose. Times are changing, but the scars of racism have not completely healed.

To be a bit more technical, *assimilation* occurs when the boundaries between what were identifiable communities, whether ethnic or racial, begin to dissolve. People who once lived apart, who never intermarried, and who did not socialize together begin to do all of these. They may once have had an uneasy relationship with neighbors who were considered inferior, but as their disparity in power erodes, they tend to feel more comfortable with each other. *Pluralism*, in contrast, refers to a situation in which communities maintain their boundaries. They continue to live, socialize, and work apart. Pluralistic groups are more concerned with honoring their diverse heritages than with adopting common ways of life. Sometimes two separate communities can be relatively equal in terms of power, but, more frequently, in remaining disconnected, they reinforce their mutual suspicions and maintain disparities in hierarchical position.

With the advent of an ideology of diversity, many Americans have come to think of pluralism as the ideal. They encourage people to celebrate their differences and assume that in maintaining them, they somehow contribute to elevating the whole. Nonetheless, the actual behavior of a majority of Americans seems to belie this. Census data reveals that intermarriage between communities is high and on the rise. People on an individual level are not only engaged in assimilation, but in amalgamation. They are biologically combining to form families that have genetic roots in many different populations. This blending has gone so far that many people are not even sure of all the groups that have joined in creating their personal heritage. Many merely think of themselves as American.

To demonstrate just how far this amalgamation has proceeded, many ethnic groups that are still regarded as pluralistic are anything but. Fully two-thirds of Italians nowadays marry non-Italians, and a majority of Jews, though they still harbor a reputation for being clannish, marry non-Jews. Even Asiatics, who are of a different race than most other Americans, intermarry in substantial numbers. For Japanese Americans, most of whom have been here for many generations, over 80 percent do so. For Chinese Americans, most of whom are of a more recent vintage, about a third do so. And although Mexicans are often considered inassimilable, approximately a third of those who move away from the Mexican border do so as well.

The exception again is African Americans. Their percentage of intermarriage is much lower than for others. Once more, racism is the explanation. It must be remembered that before the 1960s when the Supreme Court struck them down, many states had miscegenation laws. It was literally illegal for blacks and whites to have sex, let alone marry. Moreover, the social norms against intermarriage were so strong that those who violated them became outcasts from the black and white communities alike. Since then, Negroid and Caucasian marriages have been increasing at breakneck speed. They have been doubling virtually every decade, but because they began at such a low level, they still represent less than 10 percent of black marriages.

Viewed in perspective, the United States has made remarkable progress in overcoming its racist heritage. It may still have a long way to go, but it deserves the sobriquet that Ben Wattenberg has applied to it. He refers the United States as the first "universal" nation. It is surely, as he implies, the most diverse nation in the history of the world and, thanks to ongoing immigration, promises to become more diverse. More specifically, with respect to race, just as racial differences originated when human populations were separated, now that they are physically converging, it may be expected that previous classifications will fall into disuse, especially as more individuals boast a multiracial background. Tiger Woods refers to himself as Cablinasian, in deference to his combined Caucasian, black, Indian, and Asian descent. It is unclear which designations will stick in the future.

Questions

1. Can you think of any other ways in which the races differ? Which, if any of these, do you consider important?
2. What is your ethnic background? If your ancestry comes from several directions, with which do you identify? Why?
3. Which stereotypes apply to the group to which you belong? Are any of these accurate? Have any of the stereotypes changed over time?
4. Do you favor assimilation or pluralism? In which direction do you believe the United States is headed?

Selected Readings

Barone, M. 2001. *The New Americans: How the Melting Pot Can Work Again*. Washington, DC: Regnery Publishing.

Gambino, R. 1975. *Blood of My Blood: The Dilemma of the Italian Americans*. Garden City, NY: Doubleday.

McBride, J. 1996. *The Color of Water: A Black Man's Tribute to His White Mother*. New York: Riverhead Books.

Olson, S. 2000. *Mapping Human History: Discovering the Past through Our Genes*. Boston: Houghton Mifflin Co.

Sowell, T. 1981. *Ethnic America*. New York: Basic Books.

Steele, S. 1990. *The Content of Our Character: A New Vision of Race in America*. New York: St. Martin's Press.

6

Breaking the Rules: Deviance

FORMS OF DEVIANCE

They say that the exception proves the rule, and in many ways those who break the rules help us to establish what the rules are. By inducing others to sanction them, they make visible where the boundaries lie. Put another way, in doing what is not supposed to be done, they make it plain that this, as opposed to that, is not allowed. Sometimes people break the rules voluntarily and at other times they do so because they cannot avoid violating them. Either way, behaving differently from what is required elicits efforts to produce conformity.

Sometimes people who are new to sociology conclude that any sort of rule breaking constitutes deviance. They suppose that if they disobey their mothers and refuse to come to the dinner table on time, this makes them deviant. Aside from the fact that disobeying one's parents is absolutely normal, it takes more than a trivial violation of any one rule to earn this designation. Deviance consists in breaking important rules in significant ways. It is not about flouting inconsequential folkways or even modestly violating social mores. Thus, picking up a quarter from a desk where someone left it does not convert a person into a thief. Commandeering an abandoned piece of pocket change is too minor a violation to qualify as aberrant.

What, then, are the ways in which a person can be deviant? The first sort of contravention that comes to mind is crime. When people break laws, especially important laws, and/or when they do so in a habitual way, they fall into this category. Murderers are deviants. Robbers, burglars, and embezzlers are deviant. Rapists are also deviant. So are those who commit bodily assaults. Crimes against property, crimes that inflict physical injury, and crimes that break serious moral prohibitions all count as deviant. Career criminals and those whose acts outrage our sensibilities are particularly deviant.

But there are still other sorts of deviance. There is, for instance, religious deviance. If a community maintains a broad consensus regarding its religious beliefs, those who hold nonconformist convictions may be considered deviant. In a town where everyone is a Baptist, to be a Catholic might thus be deemed as going beyond the pale. To embrace Wicca or devil worship would certainly draw censure. To live in a nation where almost everyone believes in God and to proclaim oneself an agnostic, or, worse still, an atheist, is to be abnormal. In the eyes of some, it is to be so different as to not seem human. Among Muslims to become an apostate— that is, to renounce Islam and adopt another faith—is regarded as so unacceptable that the prescribed punishment is death. To abandon Allah and to become an enemy of all that is holy is thought to merit eternal damnation.

Another sort of deviance is sexual deviance. Until not very long ago public opinion in Western societies sanctioned one kind of sexual activity. Only heterosexual relations between consulting adults performed in the missionary position was considered normal. This benchmark branded those who engaged in homosexual relations as deviant and stamped other varieties of nonintercourse sex as aberrant as well. Even masturbation was regarded as unreservedly offensive. Boys who engaged in playing with their genitals were warned that they would go blind or lose their minds. Doctors literally advised parents to be on guard against onanism and to punish signs of it at their first appearance. Worse still were the so-called paraphilias. Persons who were aroused by nonstandard stimuli, perhaps by a foot fetish, qualified for this designation. They too were believed to be beyond redemption.

Nowadays, the deviance associated with chemical abuse is fairly familiar. People who overuse alcohol, or who indulge in various narcotics, may turn themselves into shells of human beings almost incapable of behaving according to the normal rules. They may be so zoned out by their drug of choice that they are too high, or too low, to deal with the real world in the required manner. Some of these individuals sit in a corner slobbering all over themselves, while others rush around madly, seeking illicit means of supporting their habits. Utterly incapable of sustaining long-term plans, many of them descend into homelessness or unintentionally succumb to a lethal overdose. In a sense engaged in slow-motion suicide, they are so needful of running away from the painful facts of their personal lives that they are oblivious to conventional obligations.

Something that may not be thought of as deviant, but that is often treated as such, is physical disability. People who suffer from epilepsy, cerebral palsy, or congenital rheumatoid arthritis may be so deformed, or so aberrant in their behavior, as to appear almost nonhuman. There was a time when those who suffered from epilepsy were regarded as possessed by the devil and, as a consequence, were shut away in compounds far from inhabited areas—much as lepers were segregated. Even people who have been paralyzed by tragic accidents get treated as different. Though their condition in no way diminishes their intelligence, or harms their hearing, when others encounter them sitting in their wheelchairs, they raise their voices or speak to their companions rather than to them. The same sort of treatment is afforded to the deaf and blind. These individuals do not behave differently from choice, but others are made so uncomfortable that their responses are equivalent to a social sanction. The deaf and blind, for example, may be so ostracized that they only feel comfortable in the company of others who are similarly impaired.

MENTAL ILLNESS

Mental illness presents a similar situation. Many individuals with mental illness are the victims of an insidious genetic disorder. Those who suffer from schizophrenia or bipolar disorder do not voluntarily adopt anomalous behavior patterns. They cannot prevent themselves from acting in ways that they too recognize as strange. Even so, they are bizarre and therefore are sanctioned. Someone suffering from an obsessive-compulsive disorder can be so irritatingly neurotic as to drive others crazy. Unlike the endearing qualities of the fictional television detective Monk, when they spend hours straightening their chairs before they sit down to dinner, onlookers are driven to distraction and may react with hostility.

Two examples of how peculiar the actions of individuals with mental illness can be took place in upstate New York several years ago. In one case a woman suffering from a borderline psychosis began to experience the pangs of cabin fever. She was victimized by long snowy winters that don't end until almost May. By the end of March, she could no longer tolerate continued confinement to her apartment. At first, she attempted to liberate herself by removing all of her clothing. When this did not work, she proceeded to head outside, where she paraded down the center of Main Street in the nude. Need it be said that bystanders found this strange? Need it be stated that shortly thereafter she was removed to the local mental hospital?

A second person, a man who had spent several years in psychiatric confinement, was discovered the day after being discharged from the hospital handing dollar bills to the chimpanzee at the local zoo through the bars of his cage. He too was returned to the hospital, where the staff quizzed him about why he would do such a weird thing. But he had a ready answer. It seems that the day before, immediately upon his discharge from the asylum, he had gone to the zoo, where the chimpanzee had instructed him to rob a nearby bank. It was after having done so that he returned to the zoo to give his mentor his cut. For him, this all made perfect sense. For others, however, it was too much to take. In their view, such flagrant rule breaking was unacceptable, whatever its cause.

Mental illness can be tragic. By interfering with normal thinking processes, it can prevent a person from behaving in ways that allow for social success. A sufferer may be perfectly cognizant of performing in ways others find intolerable, but be unable to control these aberrations. One of the more common forms of mental confusion is bipolar disorder (which used to be called manic-depression and is sometimes referred to as cyclothymia). This is a condition in which individuals suffer from wild mood swings. At one moment, they can be in the depths of a deep depression and days later be in an unnaturally ebullient, or manic, frame of mind. During the depression, he or she can be so sad that it is impossible to get out of bed. At such moments, a person completely disengages from social interaction and may refuse to perform even the simplest acts of sanitation.

During the manic phase, however, these individuals may feel wonderful. They may be brimming with confidence and energy. Ready to take on the world and to be triumphant in any endeavor, those in the grip of mania tend to overextend themselves. They are apt to engage in poorly-thought-through projects and literally spend themselves into bankruptcy. With these actions, they not only hurt themselves, but also their families. While in the manic phase, they do not realize that anything is wrong, but after it passes, must cope with the consequences of their enthusiasms. Bipolar disorders can be controlled pharmacologically, but if they are not, there can be hell to pay.

Even more serious than the bipolar disorders is schizophrenia. This condition can completely rob a person of his or her mind. Worse still, its onset is generally in the late teens or early twenties. A person who seems to have a promising life ahead is suddenly snatched away by a mysterious, almost surely genetic, disease. Schizophrenia is characterized by a number of insidious symptoms. One of these is hallucinations. A person may see and hear things that are not there. While visual hallucinations are the most disturbing, auditory ones are more common. A schizophrenic may, for example, hear voices. He or she can be plagued by what sounds like a radio in one's head. Sometimes it may be thought that these are signals coming from Mars or that they are the voices of long-dead relatives.

Another conventional symptom of schizophrenia is delusions. In this case, a person sees and hears the same things that others do, but interprets their meaning in peculiar ways. Probably the most widespread delusion is that of persecution. In its florid phase, this can rise to outright paranoia. At such moments, a person may be convinced that others are out to get him. He may believe, for instance, that others are spying on him and/or that they are concocting his murder. For the paranoid, CIA and FBI agents seem to be everywhere. Other delusions include misinterpreting what one sees on television. Someone habituated to watching soap operas may come to believe that there are hidden messages in their dialogues. Although the actors appear to be speaking to each other, they are thought to be conveying codes meant to explain what is occurring in the schizophrenic's life.

A third sort of symptom concerns the loosening of logical associations. In this case, the schizophrenic's ideas seem to collide with each other in an indecipherable hodge-podge. The individual's language becomes so incoherent as to be described as a word salad. Associations are made on the basis of sounds and not meanings; hence they reveal no consistent line of thought. When speaking to a schizophrenic exhibiting this symptom, it can feel as if there is no one at home. One's own words bounce off him or her with little effect. No wonder that this sort of behavior can be disconcerting.

Last, and more unusual, are catatonic symptoms. Catatonia is perhaps the cruelest form of schizophrenia. In its grip a sufferer stops moving. He or she goes limp and appears almost paralyzed. If the individual's arms are lifted and then dropped, such persons exhibit what is called a waxy flexibility. Typically, they stop communicating as well. They do not speak to those around them, nor respond when spoken to. So deep can catatonia be that it may take years before a person regains anything approaching a normal life. Even then, he or she is liable to have difficulty communicating. From then on, despite being medicated, a person's life chances remain restricted. Others may find him or her to be a pleasant human being, but never again will the victim seem fully human.

Nowadays there exists a cornucopia of psychoactive drugs intended to control mental illness, but contrary to pharmaceutical advertisements, these rarely return a person to a completely normal state. Moreover, many of these compounds have such disquieting side effects that those prescribed them prefer to go unmedicated. Since medication is nowadays voluntary, once discharged from a medical facility, afflicted individuals may elect to go it alone. In this instance, many descend into homelessness. Unable to care for themselves, and perhaps still suffering from symptoms such as paranoia, they elect to live in cardboard boxes rather than take a substance that makes them feel worse. Yet with deinstitutionalization still in effect, that is, with an ongoing social reluctance to hospitalize people unless they present a clear and immediate danger to themselves or others, they are free to live alfresco if they so choose.

SEXUAL DEVIANCE

Today many versions of sexual aberration are treated as mental disorders as well. The American Psychiatric Association lists a number of these under the heading "paraphilias" in its *Diagnostic and Statistical Manuals* (the so-called DSMs). One of these is fetishism. A person, such as the former agent of Marla Maples, the one-time wife of Donald Trump, may steal shoes in order to self-stimulate in their presence. Fetishists, usually males, may likewise find it impossible to become sexually aroused unless they hold a pair of female panties in hand.

Another kind of paraphilia is transvestism. Those suffering from this condition feel compelled to wear clothing representative of the opposite sex. So completely, and persuasively, can they cross dress that those who don't know them may believe that they are what they seem to be. Sometimes transvestism may merely be a matter of a man wearing his wife's underwear under a business suit. Sometimes it includes wearing wigs and make-up. Transvestism should not be confused with transsexual tendencies. Transsexuals are convinced that they were born with the wrong sort of body. They may have come into the world equipped with a male's genitals, but they are confident that they are really women. They feel so female and so fervently desire to become female that they gladly undergo drastic surgery.

Perhaps more peculiar is zoophilia. These persons eagerly engage in sexual activities with animals. Women may have intercourse with dogs or donkeys, while men have coitus with sheep. Also strange, by conventional standards, is necrophilia. This entails sexual relations with dead people. Particularly disturbing to most people is pedophilia. This involves the sexual exploitation of children. Pedophiles frequently assert that the objects of their attention desire these activities, but this is no more than wishful thinking. What is even more distressing about pedophilia is that those attracted by it have difficulty changing their orientation. Psychotherapy has been notoriously ineffective in modifying their sexual proclivities.

Less alarming, but still aberrant, is exhibitionism. These individuals find themselves stimulated by exposing their private parts to strangers. As the flashers of the world, they, unasked, strip off their clothing irrespective of the circumstances or the desires of others. On the other side of this equation are the voyeurs. These individuals find themselves excited by observing others naked. Watching couples engage in intercourse especially energizes them. They go beyond merely paying to see pornography. They are also apt to be "peeping Toms". Their greatest pleasure comes from sneaking around and surreptitiously observing people in the privacy of their bedrooms. Nowadays some voyeurs secretly place cameras in the bathrooms of attractive women so as to observe them at their leisure.

Far nastier are the sadists and the masochists. Inflicting pain on others in the course of a sexual tryst arouses the sadists. They enjoy chaining their partners up and/or whipping them as part of a shared sexual adventure. Bondage and sexual humiliation are their idea of a good time. The masochists accommodate the sadists by seeking out this sort of degradation. Being beaten turns them on, as does having a dog collar placed around their necks. Some male masochists will even hire a dominatrix to treat them as if they were small boys deserving of corporal punishment. Occasionally these activities get out of hand. People who seek arousal by coming near to suffocation now and then get suffocated unto death. Those who have grown satiated by ordinary means of torment unintentionally lose their perspective and cause, or allow themselves to be exposed to, irrevocable damage.

These paraphilias can be quite attention grabbing. For most people, they are obviously out of the ordinary. Nevertheless, despite what one may witness at the movies, these practices are not generally approved. Nowadays, of more concern, however, are our attitudes toward homosexuality. In the mid-twentieth century, almost everyone considered homoerotic behaviors deviant. Freud regarded them as evidence of neurosis, and most states enacted laws making them criminal. At the time, they were thought to be extremely rare and evidence of a grave perversion. Homosexuals were not only forced into the closet, but were their proclivities to become known, they might be subjected to blackmail.

One of the first indicators that attitudes about same-sex behavior were about to change was the work of Alfred Kinsey. A biologist by training, he turned his attention from the study of wasps to observations of human sexuality, in part because of his own nonstandard preoccupations. As a result of homosexual longings that he at first failed to recognize, he spent years prowling the forbidden districts of large cities in search of interviews with members of the gay community. He also concentrated on the sexual activities of men confined to prison. On the basis of these investigations, he came to the conclusion that fully 10 percent of American males were homosexual in orientation. When he published his findings, they scandalized his fellow citizens, but in time came to be regarded as gospel.

More recent researchers, however, suggest that only approximately 3 percent of men are gay, while 2 percent of women are lesbians. We have been able to obtain greater accuracy because the new studies have been conducted under more tolerant circumstances than Kinsey's. Today far fewer people consider homosexuality a sin. This sort of sexuality has gained so much notoriety in the media that people are more concerned with protecting the rights of gays than with converting them to heterosexuality. Many are even determined to legitimize gay marriage. Freud believed that men became homosexual because they suffered childhood trauma, but contemporary Americans are more likely to conclude that homosexuality has genetic origins.

One of the more revealing incidents in the social rehabilitation of homosexuality occurred within the psychiatric community. In the 1960s when the American Psychiatric Association (APA) decided to revise the second edition of the DSM, it assigned the task to a committee of respected psychiatrists. These men initially agreed with Freud, but when confronted by gay activists within the medical community, they realized that there was little evidence to substantiate this opinion. As a result, they put the issue to a vote of the APA membership. The question was whether homosexuality should continue to be diagnosed as a disorder. When a majority of psychiatrists voted in the negative, the once customary evaluation of this behavior pattern was altered. Eventually the former disorder was deleted from future editions of DSMs.

What this incident demonstrates is that as social norms change, what is considered deviant can also change. Psychiatrists did not discover new information about the nature of homosexuality. What occurred was a realization that a majority of them no longer considered the orientation immoral. They were no longer prepared to sanction what religious authorities had long condemned as an abomination. Homosexuality had joined the mainstream.

THE CAUSES OF CRIME

Returning now to the issue of crime—which it must be admitted is the form of deviance that most concerns sociologists—we need to inquire into the causes of serious lawbreaking. Why is it that some people engage in illegal activities, whereas others do not? Scientists, as well as laypersons, have been fascinated with this because they have been concerned with controlling crime. They have believed that if they understood why people violate the law, they could reduce law breaking. In this endeavor, they have only been partially successful.

Sociologists today entertain a variety of theories intended to explain criminality. None of these completely explicates the phenomenon, and none commands universal assent, but in combination they illuminate the whys and wherefores of crime. One of the most venerable of these theories is that of Edwin Sutherland. Referred to as the *differential association theory*, it is an updating of beliefs harbored by most parents. Sooner or later, many teenagers are confronted by mothers or fathers advising them that they are hanging around with the wrong crowd. They will be told that their friends are corrupting them and that they should seek more suitable companions. The belief is that whom you interact with influences your own behavior. Thus, if you associate with criminals, you will learn to be a criminal yourself.

The differential association hypothesis is certainly correct in some of its aspects. It is, for instance, true that one of the best places to learn how to be a criminal is in prison. Facility in some skilled crimes, such as burglary, is almost always acquired from those who are already proficient in them. So too is encouragement to engage in particular unlawful acts. This is why parole and probation officers are concerned with monitoring the social activities of those on their caseloads. Nevertheless, it is also true that people seek out their associates on the basis of their personal inclinations. They may thus decide to join a street gang because they understand full well that they may be goaded into engaging in violent activities.

A second venerable hypothesis, one connected with the name of Robert Park, is the *social disorganization theory*. Park worked at the University of Chicago during a period when the city was experiencing sizeable waves of immigration. He, among others, noted that the resultant communities experienced high levels of crime. Their young people, in particular, seemed to be attracted to illegal activities. The reason, thought Park, was that the social controls that inhibited these behaviors back in the old country had loosened. Whereas parents, grandparents, and neighbors once had the power to discourage illegal activities, in their new homeland these former authorities were no longer respected. As greenhorns, members of the older generation were unfamiliar with American conditions. They could not tell their children what was expected in this strange environs, hence their young were less inclined to listen to them. The lowered status of the parent generation also contributed to a diminution in their authority. The result was that the community became disorganized. The old rules disintegrated, while new ones had not yet evolved to take their place. This left the younger generation adrift. Thrown on to their own devices, but themselves unfamiliar with the standards of the larger community, they banded together to endorse rule breaking.

This theory is also relevant to patterns indigenous to contemporary inner cities. They are home to what might be called internal migrants. Former sharecroppers moved from the rural South to an unfamiliar urban environment, where their families underwent considerable stress. Under these conditions, unwed parenthood became common. This meant that many children were raised without benefit of paternal discipline. As a result, they too went wild, especially the teenage boys whom their overburdened mothers found difficult to control. Once more the consequence was a rash of illegality and an allegiance to gangs that disparaged the larger social consensus. In a sense, these neighborhoods also became disorganized, at least in a conventional sense.

A third theory is connected with Robert Merton. Originally called the *anomie theory*, it is currently more likely to be referred to as the *social strain theory*. A functionalist in perspective, Merton wondered what motivated criminal deviance. He came to the conclusion that what people decided to do was owed to the relationship between their personal values and the resources available to achieve these ends. If individuals accepted social values such as the desirability of possessing a large house and a fancy automobile, and they were also capable of obtaining the financial wherewithal to purchase these, they were apt to become conformists. They voluntarily followed the social rules because respecting them provided a satisfying payoff.

If, however, a person honored the customary values but did not possess the approved means of obtaining them, he might become what Merton called an innovator. One type of innovation is crime. This may be a disreputable method of acquiring what is desired, but one that may nevertheless succeed. In essence, Merton was saying that if you want valued objects but cannot afford them, you may steal them. But, claims the strain theory, you can also adopt a different stance. You might become a retreatist who rejects the standard social values as well as the conventional means of attaining these and becomes a social dropout. This sort of person could become a drifter, a street person, or an alcoholic. It is also possible to become a ritualist. This kind of person rejects social values, but accepts the normal social means. He or she does not seek conventional success, but goes through the motions anyway. He or she dresses as is expected and holds down a normal job, but conforms for the sake of conformity. On the outside all appears to be well, but on the inside the ritualist is empty and unhappy.

The next explanation of criminal deviance is the *labeling theory*. This hypothesis, often associated with Edwin Lemert, holds that crime is essentially a self-fulfilling prophecy. Those who are treated as criminals eventually become criminal. Lemert distinguishes between two sorts of deviance: primary and secondary. Primary deviance is about the initial rule violation. Lemert suggests that everyone breaks the rules from time to time. What makes a person a confirmed deviant, however, is the reaction to how this primary deviance is addressed. If one is labeled as deviant, then this may become part of a person's identity. Only after this does an individual seek to live up to the reputation that others have affixed to him or her.

Say that two boys get caught shoplifting a minor item from discount store. Assume further that one is from an upper-middle-class family and that the other comes from a lower-class family. These two teenagers are apt to be treated quite differently when they get to the police station. In both cases their parents are likely to be called, but after this their experiences will probably diverge. The parents of the middle-class adolescent will likely turn up contrite. They will apologize for what their son has done and promise to do whatever needs to be done to make certain it never happens again. The police, because they are human, may well show mercy. They will send the family home with a warning that is apt to be respected, with the final result that the teenager learns his lesson and never shoplifts again.

The son of lower-class parents, in contrast, finds that when his mother or father shows up, the parent is truculent. Such parents blame the police for arresting their son or castigate him for being a worthless piece of trash that deserves to be locked up. In either event, the police are liable to oblige by jailing their boy. This adolescent will subsequently experience himself being handled as a criminal. Like his peer, he will have committed the identical type of primary deviance, but now he will be coerced into secondary deviance. Sitting behind bars, he may come to the conclusion that if others believe he is a criminal, he might as well confirm their suspicions. If they believe that this little offense is a big deal, he will show them what a big deal really is. In this way his criminal career will have been launched.

On the basis of this purported causal mechanism, labeling theorists recommend leniency for lawbreakers. They claim that if primary deviants are not labeled by being sent to jail, they are more apt to go straight. Experience demonstrates that there is some validity to this conjecture, but less than was originally imagined. It has also been found that labeling theory does not work with mental illness. Sociologists such as Thomas Scheff argued that people became schizophrenic by being locked away in mental hospitals. They, like everyone else, behaved in a peculiar manner from time to time, but being incarcerated with crazy people ultimately drove them crazy. If they were not so labeled, they would have been able to right themselves and would not have succumbed to a full-blown psychosis. In fact, the etiology of schizophrenia seems to be largely genetic. Hospitalization may exacerbate their symptoms, but it does not create them.

Last is the *control theory* of criminal deviance championed by Travis Hirschi. Hirschi has argued that most criminals are poor planners. Unlike successful members of the middle class, they are apt to have weak impulse controls. When confronted with opportunities to participate in an unlawful act, they do not foresee their long-term impact. Instead of engaging in the sort of discipline necessary for competent self-direction, they take part in ventures that turn out badly. They lie, they steal, and they cheat; they even engage in physical violence because they do not have the emotional wherewithal to prevent themselves from getting into trouble. Says Hirschi, if we want to reduce crime, we must teach people to control their behavior. They must not only understand what the rules are—they must also acquire the internal strengths to enforce respect for them. They must themselves attain the personal discipline to refrain from temptation. Hirschi says this applies to white-collar crime as well as to violent crime.

These, then, are the major theories about why people commit crime. It should be evident that none of them covers every contingency. It should also be evident that they lead to different prescriptions as to how crime may be reduced. There are, however, other ideas regarding what needs to be done. It is to these that we now turn.

PREVENTING CRIME

Before we review methods of crime prevention that actually work, we need a brief overview of the larger territory. First, crime is international in scope. It exists in every society and has been present in every historical era. Simply having rules against certain behaviors, and even enforcing them draconically, has never been able to eradicate crime. Second, crime is not evenly distributed. Some societies are more plagued with it than others. In the contemporary world, places like South Africa and Colombia are notorious for their lawbreaking. In Colombia, this is obviously connected with the drug trade. In other places, such as Europe, it is associated with recent immigration. The United States rates higher than most countries in criminal deviance, but in recent years the rates of serious criminality have been declining. In places like Singapore, where policing is very stringent, crime is correspondingly low.

Third, crime is a young man's game. Males commit a hugely disproportionate volume of lawbreaking. They engage in upward of 90 percent of this form of deviance. In the United States, perhaps in conjunction with the rise of feminism, female criminality has been on the upswing, but it still lags far behind that of men. The greater inherent aggressiveness of males probably has something to do with this. This surely helps to explain, along with their larger size, their greater inclination toward violence. It also elucidates why young men commit most crime. The late teen years and early twenties are prime time for criminality. As men get older, certainly after they pass their mid-thirties, they are less apt to break the law. This is probably because their levels of testosterone go down. It may also be because they have acquired greater self-control.

Fourth, crime is concentrated among the lower classes. It is often asserted that crime occurs at every social level, and this is true. But the amount of crime differs dramatically according to social status. Poor people, who have less money, are not unexpectedly tempted to violate the rules and to appropriate what they desire. Socialized to conform, they are also more inclined to be rebellious. Less apt to be self-directed, they are victimized by the lack of control of which Hirschi complains. Even though the media concentrate on middle- and upper-class crime, it is far more unusual. Despite the many films in which the president of the United States is revealed to be a murderer, this has never actually occurred. Rich and powerful people are less motivated to commit crimes. By and large, having access to what they want, they realize that breaking the law places their advantages in jeopardy.

Fifth, rehabilitation programs have not been notably successful. Punishment has a terrible reputation. In a middle-class society where the corporal punishment of children is going out of style, it seems cruel to subject criminals to imprisonment or worse. It appears to make more sense to assist them in acquiring the internal controls that might permit them to manage their antisocial impulses. The problem is that the programs intended to achieve this have a terrible track record. Strategies such as "scared straight" and "boot camp" have not produced the expected effects. Young men who graduate from these programs have not been markedly successful in desisting from crime.

Although the research is controversial, some studies suggest that rehabilitation, in general, has been a failure. Without such programs, the rate of recidivism, that is, of repeat offenses, is about 70 percent. With rehabilitation, on the other hand, the rate of recidivism remains about 70 percent. There are some exceptions, but they do not bode well for the generalization of rehabilitation. To begin with, many of these programs work while in the pilot stage. When those who are highly motivated to make them succeed are in charge, their enthusiasm seems to rub off on others. Education-based programs also seem to reduce recidivism, but this appears to owe to the self-selection of their clients. Educational and therapeutic success are contingent upon personal dedication. Efforts to study or engage in personal growth that are externally prompted tend not to be energetic. The bottom line is that those who are prepared to study and/or change take advantage of opportunities, whereas those who are resistant continue to resist.

All of this may sound discouraging, but in recent years tremendous improvements have been made in discouraging crime. Since the early 1990s the rates of American lawbreaking have declined substantially. Much of this owes to the so-called "broken windows" theory. Put forward by criminologists James Q. Wilson and George L. Kelling, it was its adoption by mayor Rudy Giuliani of New York City that proved the tipping point. The broken windows theory commences with a metaphor. It asks what would happen to an abandoned building should a vandal hurl a rock through one of its windows. Supposing that no one fixed the window, after a time this would serve as an invitation for someone else to heave another rock through a second window. Soon every window in the structure would be broken and then the vandals would start on the plumbing. Eventually all of the pipes would be ripped out and the interior walls demolished by junkies seeking a safe place to shoot up. This sequence is not merely an academic conjecture. It occurred time and again in, for example, the South Bronx, where entire neighborhoods of abandoned buildings were converted into rubble.

If instead, argue Wilson and Kelling, the first window is immediately repaired, it would send a different message. Bypassers would recognize that people care about this structure and they would be more apt to respect its integrity. The moral of this tale, as drawn by Wilson and Kelling, is that if you want rules to be respected, you must enforce them. Letting things slide communicates an indifference that makes it seem that there will be no penalty for a violation. A further corollary of this conclusion is that if you wish important rules to be honored, you must also enforce the small ones. To allow the latter to be disobeyed encourages a disrespect for all rules. Potential perpetrators are led to believe that the authorities are lax and that they can get away with whatever they desire.

Giuliani took these cautions to heart and shortly after he took office sought to provide an object lesson. The violators he singled out for enforcement were the so-called squeegee men. These were largely derelicts who stood on street corners and then dashed out to clean the windows of automobiles stopped at red lights. They subsequently reached into car windows in expectation of payment for a service that was never requested. To most motorists, this reeked of extortion. Nevertheless it came to be expected and was thought to be emblematic of the city's lawlessness. Giuliani would have none of this. He ordered that the several hundred squeegee men be arrested. This was a small matter, but it was highly visible. So was arresting turnstile jumpers in the subway. Both sent the message that the days of turning a blind eye were over.

One of the places where this made the greatest difference was in the subways. Before Giuliani the trains were festooned with graffiti. Both inside and out, every square inch of these underground cars was covered with the spraypainted initials of inner-city youths. Many sophisticates alleged that this was street art. They urged that rules against it not be enforced on the grounds that this was a cheap way of encouraging the creative energies of the poor. Yet from the point of view of the passengers, this was disheartening. It made for a grubby and demoralizing atmosphere that also suggested there was no way to govern so large a metropolis. But here too Giuliani put his foot down. He decreed that the graffiti would be removed, but more than this, that when they reappeared, they would quickly be eliminated. The trains would be clean and New Yorkers would learn that the city administration respected their right not to be assaulted by visual vulgarity.

The upshot of these small interventions was that they changed larger attitudes. It was revealed that small crimes were not so small that their enforcement did not matter. Much to the surprise of many, the rates of large-scale crime went down too. Murder, in particular, was slashed by two-thirds, making New York one of the safest cities in the country. Giuliani also instituted proactive policing policies. His constabulary did not merely wait for crimes to occur. They identified at-risk neighborhoods and then sent teams of officers into these areas to catch potential perpetrators before they could do their dirty work. In the end, it was as if a cloud had been lifted off everyone's head. Taking the rules seriously made an enormous difference.

All this should be common sense, but in an era when social scientists were looking for root causes it was not. This author became aware of the power of rule enforcement when still a child. The favorite grandchild of his maternal grandmother, he was privy to a conversation in which she emphatically informed others that she would not allow a particular person to enter her home. He was, she asserted, a gonnif. *Gonnif* is the Yiddish word for thief and she was making it plain that she would not tolerate a thief around her. At this moment it also became plain to her grandson that she would cut him out of her life should he too decide to become a thief. It was simply not a career option because he knew she meant what she said.

When one enters some inner-city neighborhoods and encounters the reverse, it should not be a surprise that this has the opposite effect. When children receive approval for clever lies or when pimps are admired because their flashy clothing bespeaks monetary affluence, it should not be a shock that some children elect to follow this model. Parents who want their children to grow up to be law-abiding citizens must make evident what is approved of and what is not. In other words, if people are serious about reducing criminal deviance, they must negatively sanction that which violates social norms. To do less indicates that these are not really norms and that ignoring them is okay.

Questions

1. Are there other forms of deviance that you can think of? What are they? How serious are they?
2. Have you interacted with persons diagnosed with mental illness? What was your reaction? How did you treat them?
3. What do you believe causes crime? Which do you believe are the most significant causes of crime?
4. How would you prevent crime? What do you think of policies based on eradicating alleged "root causes" such as poverty?

Selected Readings

American Psychiatric Association, Task Force on DSM-IV. 1994. *Diagnostic and Statistical Manual of Mental Disorders*, Fourth Edition. Washington, DC: Author.

Giuliani, R. W. 2002. *Leadership*. New York: Miramax Books.

Gottfredson, M. R., and Hirschi, T. 1990. *A General Theory of Crime*. Stanford, CA: Stanford University Press.

Scheff, T. 1990. *Microsociology: Discourse, Emotion, and Social Structure*. Chicago: University of Chicago Press.

7

The Urge to Merge:
Sex and Gender

THE SEX CONTRACT

What has sex got to do with being social? Isn't it just an instinct? Isn't it merely a matter of biology? Why, then, would anyone have to be peoplized about a phenomenon that comes naturally? These are good questions, the answers to which will produce a variety of surprises. On one level, sex is surely social. In its primary manifestation, it occurs between two individuals, namely a man and a woman. On another level, it is about procreation, that is, about reproducing the population and sustaining the community. But sex is even more than this. It is also a crucial mechanism for shoring up interpersonal relationships.

Sex is one of the most important adhesives in conserving long-term interpersonal bonds. It is one of the primary forms of glue that keep people together, and, as such, can be very powerful. Like the mechanisms that underlie hierarchy, it provides some of the staying power behind crucial social structures, most notably the family. Sex is not like a handshake. It is not something that is ephemeral or can be engaged in with anybody at any time. Sex, including indiscriminate sex, has repercussions. Sex breeds loyalties, but it also arouses jealousies. So significant is it, and so significant are the things that can go wrong with sex, that every society regulates its expression. Who does what with whom is surrounded with normative controls.

The first surprise about sex is that the ways that humans do it are different than those of most members of the animal kingdom. Normally, we think of many of these other creatures as more sexually active than we are. Rabbits are infamous for copulating like rabbits, while lions can engage intercourse dozens of times a day. Nevertheless, we are more lascivious. Unlike most other mammals, human beings can partake in sex at almost any time. Unlike them, human females possess an almost unique sexual cycle. Only the bonobos, that is, the pygmy chimpanzees, rival our sexuality.

Most mammals have an estrus cycle. Their females become fertile only during certain periods of the year and it is only when they are fertile that they become sexually receptive to the male. At other times, that is, when the female is not in season, she will chase the male away. Women, in contrast, have a menstrual cycle. They become fertile once every month, but they also allow coitus when they are not ovulating. Remarkably enough, it is difficult for a human female to determine when she is capable of being impregnated. With other animals, smell and/or the color of the sexual organ are a dead giveaway that she is available. Human beings, however, must take the woman's temperature or count days since her last menstruation to establish the best moment to conceive.

These factors make human women more accessible for sex than most other animals. While bonobos outdo us—they, in fact, seem to employ sex like a handshake, having it any old time, with just about anybody, even hanging upside down from trees—we have sex more regularly than most other creatures. The question is: why? Why the menstrual cycle? Why not estrus as with most other large animals? Surely, it is not because we find sex more enjoyable than they do. Other animals too seem to take pleasure in intercourse; it is just that they do not do so as consistently as we do.

Anthropologist Helen Fisher has put forth a theory to explain this. She calls it the *sex contract*. Fisher notes that there is an important difference between humans and most creatures—that is, other than our sexual proclivities. It has to do with our offspring. Human children take much longer to mature. Young bears, for example, are on their own after two years. At this point, their mother, who has hitherto been very solicitous of their welfare, drives them away. Human mothers, in contrast, maintain close ties to their young right through their teenage years and even into adulthood. Their infants begin life nearly helpless. As a result, they must be held, fed, and protected for at least a decade and a half after birth.

The long childhoods of human offspring are atypical. Their need for socialization—that is, the requirements that they learn complex human cultures and are recruited into complicated social structures—are rigorous. It takes many years for them to understand all they must know if they are to fit into the communal life upon which their survival hinges. Indeed, it has been argued that our large human brains evolved both because we must utilize complex technologies and, even more important, to enable us to participate in multifaceted human relationships. In any event, it takes years of concentrated maternal attention before human children are capable of supporting themselves.

If this is so, the question arises as to whether mothers are capable of peoplizing their children independently. Can they, on their own, provide all the resources and all the lessons that their young require? To some extent this is possible for mothers who are embedded in a modern commercial society. They can rely on government programs to underwrite their parenting duties. But it was surely not possible in our environment of evolutionary adaptedness. Among hunter-gatherers, a woman on her own could not both protect her young and furnish them with adequate nourishment. She definitely could not go out hunting with a neonate in her arms and a toddler clinging to a leg. In short, she needed help.

The father of her children, however, had much more independence and far greater mobility. He did not have to carry his offspring to term, nor nurse them, nor worry about their welfare as they followed him about. He was free to go out hunting. He certainly had ample opportunity to meet his own nutritional needs. But what incentive did he have to share his bounty? Being bipedal, he did have two hands with which he could transport what he killed home, but why should he? What was the incentive? Says Fisher, the enticement was sex. The woman essentially made a deal with her mate. If he would share the results of the hunt with her and her children, she would provide him with sexual pleasure on a regular basis. She would be available for coitus in exchange for protection and support.

No doubt this sounds gauche. It makes intimate relationships appear mercenary, as barely a cut above prostitution. Were this all there is to heterosexual relationships, the charge would be apt, but there is more. As we will see in the next chapter, heterosexual bonds are also dependent upon love relationships. It is just that sex also matters. The need for men and women to collaborate in raising their young is so great that evolution has arranged multiple mechanisms for inducing them to do so. Moreover, sex and love can go together.

THE DOUBLE STANDARD

One of the complaints of contemporary feminists is that sexuality has been prey to a double standard. They protest that women are regarded as sex objects by men who expect chastity from their partners, yet who are free to philander as they please. This, they insist, is grossly unfair. Why shouldn't women be allowed to be as promiscuous as men? Why shouldn't women be able to have sex for the mere delight of it, then move on to someone new? On the face of it, this seems to be a good point. The problem with such an appeal is that it flies in the face of the sex contract and elementary biology. The reasons why men and women form sexual relationships, as well as the facts of human fertility, preclude the sort of casual sexuality this contemplates.

Let us begin with a mental experiment. Suppose for a moment that it is in a society's interest to regulate the number of children born. Now let us further suppose that we have two cohorts of a hundred men and women, respectively. If we exhort both of these groups to abstain from sexual activity, and are successful with 95 percent of each, how many children are liable to be conceived? If ninety-five of the women remain abstinent, then only five children may result. But if only five of the men refuse to abstain, one hundred offspring may follow. The men can impregnate multiple women, whereas the women can get pregnant only once. If one genuinely wishes to regulate the number of births, it therefore makes much more sense to restrict the sexual activities of the women.

There is also the issue that women invest much more time and energy in each of their pregnancies than do men. A woman has to carry the unborn child within her body and then nurse it after it arrives. She is also less able to conceive as many children. The record number of births for a woman is in the mid-forties, and this was only possible because it entailed a series of multiple births (e.g., twins, triplets). The record for a man, in this case a Moroccan sultan with a large harem, was in the high nine hundreds. Males, in contrast with females, even if they do not have harems, can abscond after an evening's pleasure, only to turn up in someone else's bed the next night. They can, as it is said, sow their wild oats with impunity. Women, however, have to be more careful. They must be selective in deciding who will make a good father.

The consequent attitudes of males and females toward casual sex are instructive. In an experiment originally conducted in Canada, but more or less replicated elsewhere, male and female students were requested to ask strangers of the opposite sex one of three questions. The first was, Would you like to go out on a date with me? Roughly 50 percent of both sexes answered in the affirmative to this query. The second was, Would you come up to my room?

Here approximately three-quarters of the men agreed, whereas only a quarter of the women said yes. Finally, these unknown persons were asked if they would like to have sex. In this case, almost all of the men hastened to consent, while none of the women did so. The women were all unwilling to jump into bed with a complete stranger because they understood that the outcome might be unfortunate.

This difference in attitude toward sexuality is also reflected in what males and females find attractive in members of the opposite sex. Men tend to seek qualities that are indicative of a potential partner's fertility. They are turned on by the visual characteristics of a woman. A poster of a naked female may be sufficient to arouse lust in a healthy heterosexual male. This, after all, is what pornography is about. Asked what most stimulates the male libido, many assume that it is the woman's breasts. Yet this is not the case. Attitudes toward the size of a woman's mammary glands are subject to changing fashions. Nowadays being buxom is in style; in the 1920s women tied their breasts down to make them less prominent. Men around the world, however, are stimulated by a woman's hourglass figure. A ration of 6.8 to 10 of waist to hips is perceived as particularly attractive. The reason is that this is associated with fertility. Broad hips unconsciously suggest an ability to produce healthy young.

What men find most attractive about a woman's face is also related to fertility. Large eyes, high cheekbones, ruby lips, and a small chin are all signs of youth, which in turn is correlated with fruitfulness. Other factors, such as a symmetrical face and a clear complexion, are likewise indicators of good health. These literally look beautiful, but once more they are appealing because they are signs that a woman is capable of producing healthy young. Women also understand what men are seeking. This is why they attempt to enhance their attractiveness by utilizing eyeliner to make their eyes appear larger, lipstick to make their lips seem redder, and face powder to improve their complexion while making their cheekbones more prominent. Needless to say, they in addition wear clothing that accentuates their figures. Sometimes fashions have gone to absurd lengths to draw attention to a woman's assets, as with the nineteenth-century bustle that made it impossible for them to sit down.

Women are markedly different in what they find appealing about men. How a potential partner looks is far less significant to them than are indicators that a male might be a good and loyal provider. Women may find broad shoulders and a tight derriere attractive, but they find a large wallet more so. This too sounds mercenary, but it is quite sensible. Sometimes, as in the case of high school girls who are fascinated by expensive automobiles, this propensity can be silly, but a man's earning power is not irrelevant to his ability to support a family. Having a remunerative job is an excellent indicator of his capacity to provide a comfortable home.

But a woman also wants a man who will be loyal to her and her offspring. She wants evidence not only that he can provide, but also that he will stay around to continue doing so. She will therefore be concerned with confirmation that he loves her: hence the female fascination with romance novels as opposed to pornography. Men are apt to become seriously distressed when they discover that their partners have cheated sexually. They understand that this may result in the conception of children that are not their own. Women do not have the same fears; therefore they tend to be more distraught by signs that a man is growing devoted to another woman. Cheating and then coming home is much more acceptable to them than is leaving to take up residence with a more desirable partner. This disparity has been corroborated by research on skin conductivity demonstrating that male anxieties are exacerbated by evidence of sexual infidelities, whereas women are more alarmed by emotional ones.

We even find disparities in bed. Women are much more tactile than men. Being held and physically stimulated are more arousing to them than are visual cues. Women are also more likely to want a man to tell them that they are loved. After intercourse, they wish to be assured that this is more than a one-night stand. Without ongoing evidence of a man's loyalty, they grow insecure and less satisfied. In sum, men and women express their sexuality differently. This means that if they are to relate to each other successfully, they must recognize and make allowances for these dissimilarities. They must understand that there are reasons why their standards differ and will continue to differ, despite efforts to deny their disparate motives.

SEXUAL PRACTICES

People lie about sex. Many people, especially men, are inclined to brag about their prowess, whereas others are obsessed with retaining their privacy. This has made it difficult for social scientists to establish exactly who does what with whom. Sampling errors that exaggerated the prominence of exhibitionists and those engaged in nonstandard practices hampered early attempts at research. One of the consequent mistakes was in overestimating the proportion of individuals who cheat on their partners. Even today the media make it seem that infidelities are the norm and that ordinary people hop from bed to bed with abandon. Sexual loyalties are frequently portrayed as old-fashioned. With contraceptives so readily available, it is suggested that men and women can play musical beds without ill effects. To remain faithful is portrayed as boring, unnecessary, and perhaps unsophisticated.

It once seemed that over three-quarters of all men cheated on their wives, while almost two-thirds of women returned the favor. Today the evidence indicates that this was grossly out of line. It looks as if only about 25 percent of men are unfaithful and that most of these cheaters are not serial offenders—as have been some prominent politicians. With women, only about 15 percent wander. In other words, it is decidedly not the case that everyone cheats. One of the nasty exceptions to this pattern is that approximately half of all black males are adulterous. Black women meander in line with white women's numbers, which makes their disappointment with their partners understandable. This also helps explain the lack of trust between men and women in the African American community.

Another common misconception about sexuality concerns how many partners people have during their lifetimes. The famed basketball player Wilt Chamberlain bragged that he had gone to bed with over twenty thousand women, and he furnished his bedroom in bordello style as if to prove it. Yet he is out of the ordinary. For most people, these figures are not in the hundreds or even in the scores. They do not proceed from one bar to the next intent on accumulating as many notches on the bedsteads as possible. For men, the average number of lifetime partners is in the teens, whereas for women it is less than ten. This is the case even though the age of first marriage is later than it once was and even though many more individuals are now divorced. It should also be noted that college graduates tend to have more partners than nongraduates. This is probably because they delay getting married.

Most people do, however, have sex before they get married. But much of this intercourse takes place between individuals who expect to become each other's spouses. Historically, most men had their initial sexual encounters when they were in their mid-teens. Women were more likely to guard their virginity and to take pride in it. Today the age at which women have their first experience with intercourse is about the same as it is for men. The so-called sexual revolution has indeed made it more acceptable for females to engage in unmarried coitus. It has also transformed attitudes toward unwed pregnancies. Once upon a time, this condition was so mortifying that young women were sent out of town to conceal their shame. Once upon a time shotgun marriages were likewise arranged to force the man to live up to his obligations. Moreover, the number of months at which a child was born was adjusted to make it seem that conception occurred after the marriage. This is what happened to 1950s singing icon Ricky Nelson and his wife.

Other sexual practices have also changed. Thus, masturbation is no longer considered sinful, and certainly not a medical crisis. We now understand that most people, including women, engage in self-stimulation from time to time. They even do so after marriage. We have also learned that oral sex is common. Most women engage in fellatio and a majority of men practice cunnilingus. Oddly, however, both sexes say they prefer to have oral sex performed on them rather than to perform it on their partner. Among teenagers, this act is frequently described as "hooking up" and may or may not be regarded as sex. Anal intercourse, on the other hand, tends to be frowned upon by both heterosexual males and females, and is relatively infrequent. Despite attempts to romanticize it, it is generally looked upon with disgust.

Although men like to brag about their astonishing sexual endurance (i.e., about how they typically copulate many times each night), the data belies these claims. Despite the fact that we human beings are exceptionally sexual creatures, the average number of performances per couple, per week, is about two. Furthermore, as people mature, they continue to have sex right into old age, although the number of occurrences declines to about once a week. The reality is that couples are most sexually active during the early phase of their relationship. This is when they are more likely to have multiple acts of coitus. Sex is apparently one of the mechanisms used to cement their attachment to each other during this period. The pleasure they take in providing each other enjoyment is one of the factors that bolsters their loyalty. Incidentally, one of the features that makes human sexuality unique, besides the menstrual cycle, is that couples are capable of face-to-face copulation. Because the female sexual organ has rotated forward, men and women can look into each other's eyes as they perform the sex act. Indeed, when asked which sex acts they find most appealing, participants list seeing each other undress as second.

If these figures seem disappointingly low, it should also be understood that married couples have decidedly more sex than do unmarried persons. Among other things, they do not have to go through contortions in search of a willing partner. Nor are men and women in other countries, including places with a reputation for sexuality such as France, prone to having more sex than Americans. These statistics, it must be recognized, are averages. There are always individuals who are more extreme at both the upper and lower margins of the range. Still, contemporary sex is more tame than celebrity shenanigans would lead one to believe.

Not quite considered sex, but related to it, are flirting and pick-up behaviors. These also have an interesting story to tell. One of the more enduring myths about sexuality is that men are the ceaseless aggressors. Women have frequently been portrayed as passive recipients of male attentions. They supposedly wait until the man makes the first move. This is one of the grievances of the double-standard thesis. Why, it is asked, can't women be the ones who ask men out? Why should they be compelled to sit by the telephone awaiting his call? In fact, women are very active in initiating sexual collaborations. Although men admit to thinking about sex more frequently than do women, more often than not they respond to a female's invitation.

Women, for example, often initiate flirting. They begin by smiling at a man. This lets him understand that she is interested, but can lead to mistakes on those occasions when all a woman wishes to do is be pleasant. If she intends to convey sexual attention, she will also lift her eyebrows. She then opens her eyes wide to gaze at the object of her interest. After this, as if to deny her boldness, she will tilt her head down and to the side so as to look away from the man. She may even place her hand over her mouth and giggle. Back in the old days, placing a fan over the mouth and tittering might have accompanied this maneuver.

The man does much less during this sort of episode. While he may return her gaze, and even suppose that he was the first to look, if he likes what he sees, he will emphasize his masculine strength by engaging in a chest thrust. He literally pushes out his chest to show how large and powerful it is. From this point, the couple may proceed to conversation or they may simply enjoy the implied sexuality without acting upon it.

Flirting is sometimes a prelude to pick-up behavior. Here it constitutes the initial stage of gaining the attention of a potential sexual partner. In this case too there will be mutual gazing and male swaggering. During this recognition phase, their eyes will meet to acknowledge a mutual attraction. Subsequent to this is when they begin what has been called grooming talk. Among our nearest relatives, the chimpanzees, picking insects out of one another's fur is a means of conveying friendliness. Since humans do not have much fur, meaningless conversation, perhaps about each other's astrological sign, substitutes. If this is sufficiently agreeable, the next stage entails touching. Here once more the woman is the likely aggressor. She will usually give the man permission to touch her by subtly contacting him. She may brush up against him or reach out to put a hand on his, but unless she does, most men are reluctant to attempt contact on their own. The mere idea of being shot down terrifies them.

Once she has given him the go-ahead, however, he may put an arm around her. If later asked who instigated physical contact, he will allude to this moment. It is his initiative that he recalls as decisive. If, on the other hand, he does not follow through, she, in retrospect, may indicate that she sent him signals, whereas he did not pick up on her hints. Should all go well, their growing closeness will be reflected in the synchrony of their body postures. It will be as if each is mirroring the other, with their arms and legs assuming similar positions. Thus, if they are walking together, they will be in step even though their legs are not the same length. Should this synchrony not develop, the odds that their encounter will proceed much further are not great.

ANDROGYNY?

Nowadays sociologists distinguish between gender and sex. What used to be called *sex roles* are now described as *gender roles* in recognition of the fact that the kinds of behavior assigned to individuals because of their sexual identification may have little to do with sexuality per se. As virtually everyone knows, there has historically been a division of labor between men and women. Certain jobs were believed appropriate for males and others for females. Those who crossed this divide were treated as deviant. They were typically ridiculed for not being "real" men or women. Whatever their orientations in bed, if they performed tasks generally assigned to the opposite sex, they might well become social outcasts.

Feminists, in particular, have strenuously objected to this artificial boundary. They complain that men have appropriated the best and most powerful jobs for themselves, while assigning women the leftovers. It is further asserted that this injustice has been perpetuated by male violence. Men are alleged to threaten women with rape should they have the temerity to cross into male territory. This supposedly replicates a male hegemony that originated at the dawn of agriculture when men utilized their upper-body strength to assert a monopoly over economic and political power. Nowadays, say the feminists, such exclusive control is outmoded. Men may be physically stronger, but automated machinery is as easily operated by women as men. Even long-distance trucks and remote-controlled military weapons can as successfully be handled by what has mistakenly been described as the weaker sex.

Socialization and legal obstacles are also said to have perpetuated obsolete gender roles, roles that constitute a significant element of our social structure. The sorts of relationships people are allowed to enter have thus been unnaturally, and unfairly, limited. If instead of raising boys to occupy male roles and women to perform female ones, people were permitted to do whatever they desired, the kinds of work they did would be divided fifty-fifty. Women would no longer be confined to jobs where they earned only 70 percent of what men do and men would no longer dominate political offices. Nor would women be restricted to child-rearing ghettos. Mr. Mom would become a common phenomenon, with housework more democratically allocated.

The ideal, assert the radical feminists, is androgyny. They say that gender differences beyond those of sexual plumbing should be abolished. Sociologists such as Judith Lorber agitate for the entire disappearance of gender roles. They claim that gender should have nothing to do with the sorts of tasks people perform. According to them, boys and girls should be raised the same way. Once they are, it will be revealed that ostensible differences in personal qualities such as aggressiveness are merely artifacts of the male hegemony. It will become evident that neither gender is smarter or more creative than the other. All human beings will be exposed, first and foremost, as human.

At first blush, this sounds democratic. It seems to be in accord with our Declaration of Independence in implying that all people were created equal. Nevertheless, an assertion of equality does not of itself demonstrate equivalence. Moral parity should not to be confused with organic sameness. To state that there are no differences between men and women, except for their sex organs, does not prove there are no biologically based distinctions. Nor does it establish that such differences as do exist might not underlie a gender division of labor. The radical feminists assert that nurture, not nature, is the cause of all the variations that currently exist. They maintain that if we change our modes of socialization, and eliminate discriminatory legislation, androgyny will result. They are unimpressed by the universality of gender-based divisions of labor. That no known society has ever been without such distinctions strikes them as evidence of the extent of male turpitude, not of inborn disparities.

In fact, there seem to be many differences between men and women beyond the obvious sexual ones. The more research that is done on these matters, the more completely these disparities have been documented. Before elaborating upon them, however, it is essential to assert that these differences are not absolute. It is not as if men are all one thing and women all another. What one discovers is overlapping normal curves. The averages for men and women tend to be different, but it is not as if all men possess more of a quality than all women, or vice versa. Consider height. On average, American men are over five inches taller than American women. But this does not mean that all men are taller than all women. Even the most casual observation indicates that some women are quite tall, while some men are unusually short.

Yet another caveat is applicable here. Such differences that do exist are frequently exaggerated by social factors. Certainly we see this in the case of height. Because men tend to seek out women who are shorter than themselves, while women conversely search for men who are taller than they are, couples are not matched at random with respect to size. As a result, more often than pure chance would suggest, the man will be the taller of a bonded pair. The same occurs with respect to other characteristics. Thus women tend to gravitate to men who are more aggressive than they are, whereas men seem to prefer women who are more nurturing than themselves.

There is also the fact that socialization may reinforce genetically grounded variations. Those who believe in androgyny are quite correct in maintaining that boys and girls are raised differently. Besides the traditional blue for boys and pink for girls, there are more basic ways in which young children are treated differently. Baby girls, for example, are more apt to be picked up and comforted when they cry. Boys are likely to be toughened up by being left alone. Similarly, boys are more likely to be given guns with which to play, while girls receive dolls. Nonetheless, efforts to equalize these practices have infamously failed. Boys who are given dolls tend to smash them together rather than play house with them. Likewise, if deprived of guns, they utilize sticks or even fingers so they can play at making war.

Turning to specific differences and correlating them with observable physiological disparities, we discover that the way that men and women think varies. The genders may not differ in intelligence, but they do differ in how they apply their intellects. For starters, the corpus callosum is larger in women than in men. This means that the two halves of the female brain are tied together better than those of the male brain. This disparity is reflected in brain scans that demonstrate divergent methods of problem solving. When men and women are given exactly the same problem to unravel, multiple centers in both halves of the female brain light up. With men, in contrast, only one area in one of the hemispheres tends to be activated. Male thinking thus tends to be more specific, whereas that of females is more generalized.

One of the behavioral correlates of this physiological difference is multitasking. Women are much better at juggling several simultaneous tasks than are men. In an office setting they will keep a number of machines operating at once, whereas men tend to go from one to another in sequence. This difference also seems to be the source of allegations of feminine intuition versus male logic. When women say that they have a feeling that something is true, but cannot specify what it is, this may because they are simultaneously processing information coming from a variety of directions. Men, in contrast, are more linear in their thinking. Because their brains go step by step, they are better able to articulate the logic of their conclusions. This does not make one form of thinking better than another, merely different.

An area in which women are definitely superior is that of verbal skills. The part of the brain that processes language is on average about 20 percent larger in women than in men. No wonder that girls do much better than boys in verbally related school subjects. No wonder, too, that women talk more than men. Within the domestic sphere, wives talk almost twice as much as their husbands. This is why they have a reputation for being nags. It is also why men are more likely to be described as the strong, silent type. Nevertheless, men are more verbal in the public sphere. In this domain, they assert their leadership by articulating what they believe others should do.

Men, in contrast with women, tend to be superior in spatial and mathematical tasks. They find it easier to visualize objects in three dimensions. Among the feminists it has become conventional to disparage this purported skill. Hence it is that a myriad of jokes ridicule men for failing to ask directions when they get lost. Nonetheless, a closer inspection demonstrates a difference in how the genders deal with directions. Men instruct other men to travel such and such a distance before turning west, whereas women prefer instructions in terms of landmarks. They are more comfortable being told to turn left at the big church with the white steeple.

Two experiments illuminate these disparities, and perhaps explain their origin. At the University of Rochester some years ago researchers took advantage of the areas terrible weather. Given the large volume of snow that falls annually, the school has many underground tunnels. It was therefore possible to take male and female students, blindfold them, and then bring them below street level. The next step was to walk the students around the tunnels and after awhile to ask them in which direction various landmarks were to be found. The females tended to be totally confused by this exercise, whereas the males could more or less indicate where the library, for example, was located.

A very different outcome occurred at another university, where male and female students were ushered into what they were told was a waiting room. This tiny space was furnished with a single chair, a desk, and a bulletin board. On the desk and board were placed many small items. After a couple of minutes the subjects were removed to a second room where they were asked to enumerate what they had seen. Under these conditions it was the males who had the most difficulty. They could usually recall two or three items at best. The females, however, could rattle off a long list of what was in the original room.

So what is the meaning of all this? One theory is that these observations indicate differences that go back to our hunter-gatherer days. In the environment of our evolutionary adaptedness, it is clear that a gender-based division in which men were the hunters and women the gatherers prevailed. Hunters, of course, need good three-dimensional abilities. If they are to kill prey bounding through trees, they must be able to judge where and when these creatures will emerge. Gatherers, in contrast, must be able to locate small items, such as onion roots. They need to remember where these are if they are to extract them.

Other gender differences may also hark back to our evolutionary roots. For instance, the fact that women talk more than men may relate to the fact that silence is frequently essential during the hunt, whereas gatherers benefit from speaking out loud. When they make noise, this might frighten away animals that could otherwise endanger their children. Similarly, women's superior fine motor dexterity is better suited to manipulating small items, whereas men's superior gross motor dexterity, including their greater upper-body strength, is more appropriate to the rigors of the hunt.

Perhaps the most contentious allegation about the nature-based differences between men and women relates to the purportedly greater aggressiveness of men. Before going further, however, it is essential to assert that women too are aggressive. We human beings are an aggressive species. Yes, men like to be winners and will assert themselves so as to come out on top, but so will women. Once more we are dealing with overlapping normal curves. The differences between the genders are relative, not absolute. Still, efforts to deny discrepancies in aggressiveness have never succeeded. Even noted psychologist Eleanor Maccoby back in the 1950s was forced to admit that these existed. We can actually detect them in infants, before socialization has had a chance to operate. When set on the same blanket, little boys are more apt to give little girls a shove than the other way around.

This said, sociologists have long made a distinction between instrumental and expressive orientations. Men have been demonstrated to be more instrumental, that is, to be especially concerned with completing a task. Women, in comparison, are more apt to be concerned with the emotional dimensions of what is occurring. It is not that women do not seek to achieve goals. They do. It is rather that in a group of people they are more attuned to maintaining peaceful relationships than are men. Men tend to be more single minded; hence if confronted with a problem, they will likely suggest a way to overcome it. Women, told of the predicament another person is experiencing, are more inclined to express sympathy. They are more apt to commiserate with the sufferer than offer a solution.

This difference is expressed in a number of ways. For example, in team sports such as basketball, male players are liable to get very angry with teammates who blow an easy play. Women players, in comparison, are more likely to be supportive and to assure the miscreant that she will get it right the next time. Turning to the home, it is the mother who usually provides solace to children distraught over an unexpected defeat. It is also the woman who is likely to send out birthday cards to relatives—including those of her husband. She also makes the telephone calls intended to maintain family contacts. This is why the woman is generally considered the hub of the family.

This is also why men do not cry in public. Feminists once urged men to let their tears flow on the grounds that there was nothing shameful in exposing one's sensitivities. Most men understood, however, that openly crying over their defeats was an invitation for other men to pick on them. Once perceived as weaker and less aggressive than their rivals, they were regarded as easy targets who could be thrust into positions of inferiority. Women, in comparison, are liable to be more sensitive to the emotional states of others. They are, in fact, better at noticing emotional moods. Hence it is that men will often consult their wives about the emotional currents swirling about a party they have just attended.

And herein lies the connection between aggressiveness and an instrumental orientation. Men understand that if they are to be powerful, that is, if they are to exercise leadership in group projects, they must come out on top in tests of strength. When challenged by other men, they cannot afford to commiserate with rivals who also desire to win. They must instead be able to intimidate these others into submission. Men who are perceived as winners, especially in tasks as inherently dangerous as hunting, must be prepared to take risks. They have to court defeat energetically in the hopes that they will succeed and be rewarded with communal respect. Only in this way can they protect the community by organizing group activities. This is as valid in today's corporate world as it once was on the hunt.

For women, however, the center of their universe has historically been the family. Their superior emotional skills have generally been applied to raising their children within a supportive milieu. Women have usually been described as more nurturing than men. Certainly, young children tend to prefer their high-pitched voices and tender touch. It is thus they to whom young children turn when they have skinned their knees and crave a healing kiss. This is also why men who have been mortally wounded on the battlefield will cry out for their mothers—not their fathers.

All told, a dispassionate review of the nature of men and women demonstrates a host of differences. While these are not all of equal import, they do suggest that men and women might make different choices as to what they consider important. Women, for instance, are much more likely to be devoted to interacting with their children than are men. Anyone who has worked in an office will have run into knots of women ogling over a coworker's newborn. They will also have noticed that women who rise to top executive posts are generally unmarried, or at least childless. Mothers are more apt to take time off to attend to a sick child and are less willing to take business trips that separate them from their offspring.

EFFECTS OF THE INDUSTRIAL REVOLUTION

If all of these differences between the genders exist, how is it possible that they have been so adamantly denied? How can androgyny be held up as an ideal when it so clearly flouts observable distinctions? The answer can be found in the consequences of the Industrial Revolution. There was a time two or three hundred years ago when the gender division of labor was not controversial. Both men and women understood that there were differences, yet neither gender objected. Not only did these distinctions seem natural, they were judged as necessary.

Back then most men were farmers and most women were homemakers. Men worked in the fields from sunrise to sunset performing heavy physical labor. Women had no wish to join them in this, for they had a myriad of tasks to perform in the house. At the time it was understood that a woman's work was never done. Not only did she have to care for the children in an age before compulsory education, but she had to cook the family meals in a fireplace. More than this, she was responsible for providing the family with clothing. This meant that that on laundry day she began the day by making the soap. It also meant that she weaved the cloth that she later sewed into the homespun clothing for her brood. Women were then referred to as the *distaff sex* because if they had nothing else to do, they walked around carrying a small spinning wheel in their hands called a distaff.

Under these conditions, both men and women understood that they could not survive without the contributions of the other. Those who remember Walt Disney's television saga about Davy Crockett may also remember that Crockett's wife dies early on, leaving him with two young children. In the Disney version of his life Crockett simply goes on with his adventures. In reality, he remarried with weeks. His new wife was a recent widow who needed a man to feed her and her young, while he required a woman to raise his children and care for his home. Both parties accepted this, because they had little choice. But more than this, each knew that he or she would be respected for what was provided. The woman, in particular, did not feel like a second-class citizen because she was as vital to the family's survival as was her husband.

Then came the Industrial Revolution. In time, this impelled many men to leave the farm to work in the factory. Now he was said to bring home the bacon, albeit in the form of money. Meanwhile his wife continued to stay at home. But her life also changed. Soon she was surrounded by labor-saving machinery. She acquired a stove, a refrigerator, and in due course a microwave. She also found it possible to purchase soap and factory-made clothing at the local store. Ivory even advertised that its soap was superior to hers in that it was 99.44 percent pure.

By the 1950s industrialization had progressed so far that stay-at-home women often had little more to do than watch soap operas on television. With this development, women found their labors less respected. They understood that their husbands did not need their services as much as they once did. They could, after all, feed themselves in restaurants or with frozen TV dinners. It also began to occur to women that they were now free to obtain jobs of their own.

They did not have to be dependent on their husbands if they did not wish to be. They too could be independent.

In essence what occurred is that the traditional male roles remained viable, whereas those of women were undercut. This left women envious of men. No longer feeling important, they demanded something more. Looking around for an alternative, the feminists decided that women should enter the male roles. Since they too could perform these, why shouldn't they claim the authority and esteem that went with them? In other words, the way to rescue women from their ennui was to abolish the traditional division of labor.

Part of this prescription is undoubtedly correct. Everyone, both male and female, needs to be respected. Everyone needs to make contributions that others find important. The error was in assuming that the only way to achieve this was by denying the differences between the genders. What is apparently occurring is not a dissolution of the division of labor, but its reorganization. There still remain gender-based differences in what men and women do, it is just that these differences have changed. Once physicians were exclusively male; now the profession is in the process of including more females. Once real estate agents were all male; now a large proportion are female.

But this misses important distinctions. Female physicians tend to concentrate on family medicine, whereas males predominate in surgery. Likewise, female real estate agents sell private homes, whereas males dominate the commercial market. A close inspection reveals that the choices people make tend to be related to their abilities and interests. Women tend to prefer jobs grounded in nurturing and family, whereas men gravitate to those that require spatial aptitudes and aggressive inclinations. Women are more inclined to cooperate; men, in contrast, are inclined to compete.

Gender reformers once recommended that people make occupational choices independent of their gender. They assumed that this would lead to a 50/50 division. This does not seem to be what is occurring. Left to their own devices, more women prefer to teach in grammar school, while men prefer to work construction jobs. One sees these proclivities operating even at the college level, where English departments are dominated by women while engineering departments remain a masculine realm. What people must now ask is whether men and women will be permitted to follow their biologically determined desires, or if they will be coerced into an artificial version of equality.

Questions

1. What else attracts men and women to each other? Are these factors related to the need to reproduce or to the sex contract?

2. Is the double standard outmoded? Should dating practices be reorganized so that women are as assertive as men?

3. Do you believe in androgyny? What would a world without a gender-based division of labor look like?

4. Should affirmative action be used to equalize the sorts of work men and women perform? Should it be employed to change domestic roles?

Selected Readings

Farrell, W. 2005. *Why Men Earn More*. New York: Amacom.

Fisher, H. 1982. *The Sex Contract: The Evolution of Human Behavior*. New York: William Morrow and Co.

Michael, R. T., Gagnon, J. H., Laumann, E. O., and Kolata, G. 1994. *Sex in America: A Definitive Study*. New York: Warner Books.

Moir, A., and Jessel, D. 1989. *Brain Sex: The Real Difference between Men and Women*. New York: Delta.

Sommers, C. H. 1994. *Who Stole Feminism: How Women Have Betrayed Women*. New York: Simon & Schuster.

Intimacy and Its Discontents: Family Life

THE ADVANTAGES OF MARRIAGE

Some say marriage is obsolete. They herald the arrival of an interpersonal diversity where any sort of intimate relationship is as good as any other. For many, the ideal is free love. They claim that marriage ties people down, that it is tantamount to slavery and ought to be passé in our modern era. Women, in particular, are said to be oppressed by matrimony. There is no good reason why they should subject themselves to masculine bondage when they are perfectly capable of caring for themselves and their children. For these critics, love is a myth. It is a fable told to induce people to relinquish their independence and accept domestic misery.

Nevertheless, the overwhelming majority of people still get married. They may not remain married forever, but they do give the institution a try. Most people also dream of finding true love. They hope one day to find a soul mate with whom they will be able to share conjugal bliss. As a consequence, dating services thrive, as do a plethora of heterosexual entertainments. Though it is true that fewer people live within the traditional nuclear family, this is primarily because they get married later, more frequently divorce, and live longer so that their children have moved out and/or one spouse has survived the other.

Sociologist C. J. Waite has taken a hard look at marriage and concluded that married people are better off on a variety of dimensions compared with singles. For starters, they are healthier. It has long been recognized that men derive a health bonus from marriage, but it has been assumed that women do worse. Men do, in fact, gain more. Their life expectancy increases by four or five years. This seems to be because on their own they take foolish risks. They ride motorcycles and jump out of planes. They also stay away from doctors. Once married, however, their wives pester them to take better care of themselves. Wives oversee their husbands' diets and remind them that if they get hurt, they won't be able to maintain their family responsibilities. Women themselves don't do badly in marriage, although they gain less than an extra year of life. This is because they are already taking good care of themselves prior to tying the knot.

Couples are also better off economically after marriage. It used to be said that two can live as cheaply as one. Though this is not exactly true, they can do better than each on their own. Not only may there be two incomes per household, but living together means that many costs do not have to be duplicated. A married couple needs a bigger refrigerator, but only one, not two. Similarly they require more space, but not double what they required while living separately. It is even possible to economize on food when buying in bulk and to reduce per capita utility bills when lighting the same rooms and watching the same TV.

Another benefit of marriage is emotional companionship. Not only do married couples have more sex than singles, but, in the healthier relationships, they have someone with whom to share their lives. Being lonely can cause significant emotional stress. Having someone who cares about one's fate, as well as someone about whom to care, furnishes a haven in a heartless world. Among other things, it provides an outlet at the end of the day where a man and a woman can talk out their respective experiences. In so doing, they need not feel that they are on their own in fending off a sometimes hostile universe.

Then there are the children. Marriage as a social institution is more concerned with providing stability for them than their parents. But adults too benefit from being parents. Despite the demands made of them, and the emotional wear and tear that caring for youngsters can impose, most mothers and fathers gain more from their offspring than they give. Psychologist Erik Erikson has written about the importance of generativity to the successful life. Being able to contribute to the perpetuation of our species is inherently fulfilling. But more than this, the love and respect of one's children, even when these offerings are unspoken, can imbue life with meaning.

As for the children themselves, being raised within a loving family is one of the best guarantees of their fulfillment. On virtually every measure available, individuals who grow up in two-parent families do better than the children of divorce or of single-parent households. They perform better in school, staying longer and obtaining better grades. Their health, including their mental health, is also better. They have fewer heart attacks and are less inclined to depression. They are thus happier and live longer. Economically they are likewise better off, and when they get married, they are less apt to divorce. More trusting of members of the opposite sex, they are more comfortable with conjugal intimacy. The children of stable marriages also feel more secure. They feel protected and less alone in the universe.

Utterly remarkable is the degree to which marriage has come to be considered irrelevant for children. In the past, out-of-wedlock births constituted about 3 percent of white births and 5 percent of black births, but by the end of the twentieth century these figures had jumped to about 23 percent for whites and nearly 70 percent for blacks. This is nothing less than a national crisis, especially considering that the children of the poor are most likely to be affected and therefore are less able to climb out of poverty. Those who are anxious to aid the downtrodden would thus do well to contemplate how marriages might be strengthened.

COURTSHIP

Those who disparage marriage frequently dismiss these unions by conflating them with a piece of paper. Why, they ask, can't people just live together? Why do they require an artificial legal document? In fact, marriage is about commitment. It is about establishing an emotional bond between two people and socially affirming this attachment in a public ceremony. Back in the hippie era, people experimented with trial marriages and open marriages. They assumed that if they lived together before making their merger official, they would learn enough about each other to avoid later mistakes. Experience has, however, demonstrated that this was a fatuous hope. Couples who cohabit for considerable periods of time are much more likely to divorce should they subsequently wed. Apparently, those who decide to marry before playing house are more committed to the institution and are therefore more likely to work at making it succeed.

Similarly, swinging couples who openly engage in infidelities have more fragile unions. Advocates of wife swapping once bragged that sexual variety kept their marriages fresh, but this was always more propaganda than reality. Because sexual adventurism is tantamount to disloyalty, it has adverse consequences for interpersonal trust. Yet trust is essential for marital commitment. Without it, the partners can never be sure where they stand. Because intimacy makes individuals vulnerable, they inadvertently expose themselves to a multitude of injuries, large and small.

How, then, do individuals decide with whom to establish a long-term relationship? How can they determine which person would make an appropriate mate? And how do they create the stable attachment at the core of a good marriage? For most of history these challenges have been left to outside forces or to chance. Thus, a couple's parents once arranged most marriages. They evaluated the appropriateness of a particular alliance and demanded compliance. In the modern era, however, men and women perform these services on their own, yet they venture into these brambles at the mercy of a host of romantic fantasies. Many expect that one day lightning will strike—that when their eyes meet the one perfect person for them, they will instantly recognize each other.

The realities are far more complex and less idealistic. To form a solid relationship, the parties must first select an appropriate other and then navigate the uncertain currents of a courtship process. Out of the many millions of potential partners, they will investigate only a few and go into depth with even fewer. They begin with what Willard Waller described as rating-dating procedure. During this period, they will go out with a variety of persons and compare them as to their relative suitability. Eventually they may decide to explore a deeper alliance with one individual rather than with others.

It might be assumed that daters are searching for the best possible partner, but this is not so. What they are seeking is someone on a level comparable to their own. Intimacy, especially wedded intimacy, is about being comfortable with another human being. To live contentedly with another individual one must be able to relax in his or her presence. One must be able to be oneself. If the other person is perceived as superior, a person may feel compelled to live up to this standard. Yet this can entail putting on an act and never sharing one's real self with this other. Besides being emotionally draining, such tensions are hardly satisfying.

Nevertheless, two people do not have to share exactly the same strengths. One can be rich and the other beautiful and still conclude that neither is better than the other. There are, however, several dimensions in which people should be comparable. One of these is intelligence. Contemporary American mythology suggests that men are seeking beautiful but simple-minded women—the legendary ditsy blond. But how much fun would it be to be saddled with a partner who does not understand what one is saying? Conversely, how pleasurable would it be to be regarded as an idiot by someone who is intellectually superior? In reality, married couples are quite similar in their mental endowments.

Another dimension on which successful couples tend to be similar is their values. If one believes in honesty, so should the other. A liar coupled with a truth-teller is a partnership liable to engage in never-ending controversies. Married pairs should also have similar attitudes toward creating a family. If one wants children, but the other does not, they too will be plagued by interminable squabbles. On the other hand, religious differences are generally of less importance. Given that their attitudes toward religiosity are comparable, they can contentedly subscribe to different denominations. Social class dissimilarities, however, are more difficult to reconcile. Because social class is so closely related to lifestyle, absent homogamy there may be serious clashes regarding their daily routines.

In any event, when individuals locate someone who might make a potential mate, they must investigate further. Love at first sight is largely for storybooks. While lust at first sight is possible, love entails a relationship with a particular person and this is difficult without knowing the person. This is why dating typically entails first going out to dinner. Sharing a meal with someone provides an opportunity to exchange information about each individual's background. Because they are liable to start out as strangers, they will not be able to decipher each other's attitudes and social attachments merely from sight.

The first order of business is therefore biography swapping. Each tells the other stories about his or her past and communicates hopes and fears. In the beginning, these materials tend to be flattering. As per Goffman, one wants to make a good impression on this other person. Yet the time will come for greater honesty. Since none of us is perfect, an accurate mutual understanding eventually requires the disclosure of embarrassing details. This, however, needs to be achieved carefully and in a balanced manner. If one party provides the other with what amounts to a stick with which one might be beaten around the head and shoulders, it is essential that this be reciprocated with something equivalent. If it is not, it will be impossible for mutual trust to develop.

Shared trust is absolutely critical to successful intimacy. Intimate relationships are inherently dangerous. When people get close to each other, both physically and emotionally, they are in a position to inflict terrible pain. Two people who occupy the same bed can literally disfigure one another during the night—most men shudder at the vengeance perpetrated by Lorena Bobbitt. But the emotional damage can be worse. People who live in close proximity get to know each other's weaknesses. They learn where the other person's buttons are located and they are close enough to push them should they feel a desire for retaliation.

This is the reason that courtship invariably entails testing a potential partner's trustworthiness. Merely observing the other's dependability is insufficient. Circumstances must be arranged such that one can evaluate how the other will respond. Can the partner keep a secret? What better way to tell than by disclosing a secret. Does the other lose his temper when frustrated? One way to find out is to arrange a frustrating experience. Perhaps the two can take an extended automobile trip. This is usually so stressful that something undoubtedly goes wrong. Is this other respectful of one's needs? What happens when the pair goes out to a good restaurant? Does she order the most expensive item on the menu? Does he embarrass her by boisterously berating the waiter? Some tests of trustworthiness can be quite creative. When Maria Shriver was dating Arnold Schwarzenegger her family advised her to buy him a dog.

The theory was that the way he treated this animal would be a good indicator of how he might later treat her or any children they might have.

Should all go well—that is, should this other person prove both interesting and trustworthy—the next phase of the courtship process is liable to be infatuation. Many people confuse infatuation with love itself. When people are infatuated, they feel wonderful. It is as if they are floating on air. Their love object appears to be perfect and they regard themselves as luckiest person alive. When infatuated, couples call each other by pet names and during meals they feed each other small morsels of food. Should they turn on the radio and listen to the love songs, these now make sense. One of the melodies may even be adopted as their song. From the perspective of others, they seem to glow. From their own perspective, some of the lyrics from *My Fair Lady* apply. As the young man infatuated with the title character sings: "I have often walked down this street before, but the pavement always stayed beneath my feet before. Now all at once am I several stories high knowing I'm on the street where you live." They too feel several stories high.

During the infatuation phase, couples are convinced that they can live on love. They are certain that their rapture will last forever, that no two people have ever loved this deeply and hence that their bond can never be severed. And yet this feeling does not last. Sooner or later something goes wrong. He wipes his nose with the sleeve of his coat. She takes too long to prepare for an evening out. Whatever the incident, something that in the heat of their passion would be overlooked is suddenly annoying. Quite unexpectedly, a lover's quarrel erupts. Without warning an act that feels like a betrayal intervenes and the aura of perfection is dispelled.

Had this provocation occurred at the beginning of their relationship, it would probably have occasioned its dissolution. After the infatuation, however, the parties stick around to work through their differences. And this is the function of the infatuation. It is all about creating an emotional attachment. The period of disorientation that the couple traverses alters their priorities. They begin to incorporate each other into their respective life spaces. Now it becomes important to them to reconcile their disagreements so that they can continue to collaborate on joint projects.

At this juncture, the pair enters what is probably the most crucial stage of the courtship process. It is the lengthiest phase, the one most closely associated with cementing their commitment. This is the negotiation stage. No matter how well suited a couple, there is no such thing as a perfect fit. There are always areas in which two people will differ and must reach as agreement on how to proceed. They must find some kind of compromise that allows each to receive part of what they desire. One-sided settlements that satisfy only one are fraught with grievances. These are merely a prelude to perpetual friction.

Among the issues that must be decided, especially after people take up residence together, are innumerable matters, small and large. Little things such as who will sleep on which side of the bed or how many towels should be purchased for the bathroom can divide the couple. So may bigger issues such as whether and when to have children or if the pair should move to accommodate the job of one, but not the other. Also on the agenda may be when to visit the in-laws, at which hour dinner should be served, or the best color for the living room carpet. Some of these can be so contentious that they will take days, weeks, or even months to settle. In any event, successful couples have to discover methods for resolving disputes that work for them. With no umpire around to mediate their quarrels, they have to develop negotiation techniques acceptable to both.

Some people believe that love solves all problems. They assume that once they commit to the perfect mate all their other difficulties will dissipate. The leftover pains from their childhoods will be dispelled, while the uncertainties of an unclear future will lose their terrors. This too, of course, is a myth. In the Bette Midler song "The Rose," she denies that love is exclusively for the lucky or the strong. Yet this may be the sad truth. One of life's most painful paradoxes is that those who could most benefit from love are the least likely to get it. Those whom fate has deprived of love when they were young are less apt to have acquired the characteristics necessary to attract love as adults.

One of the saddest aspects of schizophrenia is that it strikes young people in the first flush of adult optimism. Either in college or looking forward to it, they are suddenly struck down by a mysterious malady that requires hospitalization in a mental facility. Not only are their occupational aspirations thrown askew, but now they must question whether they will ever find true love. Who, after all, would want a relationship with a schizophrenic? After a period of despair many come to the realization that such a person could only be another schizophrenic. At this, one often observes the flowering of hospitalized romance. Two inpatients find each other and in the course of time pledge each other eternal fealty. They vow to be there for each other and to set up a household in which they support their respective aspirations.

For most, however, there is a rude awakening upon reentering the community. They soon discover that this other person, the one who promised to meet all their needs, fails to deliver. Instead of assuaging their pains, this other begins making impossible demands. What they learn is that their professed partner is as needy as they are. Each hurts so much that they are better at taking than giving. Yet intimacy is about being able to do both. It requires the personal maturity to make concessions and to be sensitive to another person's vulnerabilities. Those who are hurting, and/or those who have a hole in their hearts thanks to a barren childhood, have a difficulty doing either. On the contrary, they tend to be desperate. They can be so demanding, and so clingy, that those who are capable of furnishing love are driven away.

Individuals who never grow up, that is, those who never mature, make terrible negotiators. They don't make good bargains so much as demand tender loving care from others. Moreover, they are unskilled at recognizing their personal needs or deciphering those of a potential partner. Eager to be saved by love, they never realize that people can only save themselves. It never occurs to them that growing up is something a person must largely do on his or her own. Others may help, but they can only do so for those capable of benefiting from help. The first step to a successful courtship may thus be to get in touch with oneself and to take those measures necessary to become a grown-up. Intimacy takes the courage to face life, but this bravery is a product of becoming fully adult.

MARRIAGE

Even when a courtship proceeds to a positive conclusion, this is but the beginning of long journey. Marriage takes work. Problems regularly crop up that must be addressed and resolved. There are always moments of frustration when one or both of the partners are tempted to throw up their hands and discard a person whom at this instant is not loved. Unconditional positive regard is all well and good for textbooks. In real life, people get angry. Their warm feelings are conditional on this other person behaving in a reasonably satisfying manner. Thus, if they are to remain married, they must make an effort to fix what is broken. Yet this truly can be work. It can be a struggle to do what at the moment one does not want to do.

In the modern world, couples frequently begin with a relatively egalitarian union. Being in love, they believe in fairness. They do not want to exploit a cherished other. Since most contemporary marriages are dual-career affairs, both partners will also be working. This means that both must meet demands emanating from outside their household and thus will have less time and energy available for those arising within it. At the end of the day, both are liable to be tired and perhaps out of sorts. The last thing they need is more work.

Times have changed, but most of us are aware that a well-understood division of labor once characterized the traditional marriage. The woman was responsible for preparing the meals, cleaning the house, and caring for the children. The man, in turn, was accountable for providing a good income, making household renovations, and mowing the lawn. Each knew his or her place and respected that of the other. If he entered her kitchen, he knew that she had a right to drive him out. If she disturbed him in his workshop, she did so with trepidation. There was little temptation to poach on the other's territory.

Nowadays this partition of duties seems quaint. It appears to violate our aspirations toward equity. Nevertheless, a marital division of labor still makes as much sense as does an industrial one. In industry, separating jobs leads to greater efficiency. In a marital household, it reduces frictions. When a man and a woman aim at precisely the same goals, they are liable to compete to determine who is in charge and/or who will come out ahead. Unfortunately, if one is successful, the other may be comparatively less successful. They may then be like a Hollywood couple in that if one becomes a star, and the other does not, the resultant envy can precipitate their rupture. On the other hand, if one is acknowledged as having superior mechanical gifts, whereas the other is recognized as being a better writer, each can take pride in the other's accomplishments without fearing that their own will thereby be diminished. Head-to-head competition can be fatal to love, whereas cooperation improves the prospects of both. When each can freely root for the other, both are able to enjoy the fruits of their mutual affection.

The difference between the past and the present is that the traditional household division of labor is no longer viable. Because most couples now work, it usually does not make sense for the husband to expect the wife to have dinner waiting when he comes through the door. Instead, the contemporary couple is compelled to arrange a division of labor that works for them. Perhaps he will be the one who does most of the cooking and a preponderance of the grocery shopping. Perhaps she will repair the broken appliances or mow the lawn. A strict gender-based allocation of tasks based on traditional models no longer applies. What is necessary instead is that the two negotiate an arrangement with which both are comfortable. This way each will know the domains in which he or she is in charge and will be able to defer to the respective perquisites of the other.

These ongoing negotiations are facilitated if the partners are likewise skilled at role-taking. If they can imaginatively place themselves into the shoes of the other, they can make allowances for this other person's demands. He may, for instance, realize that she is also fatigued after putting in a long day at the office and will therefore take up some of the meal preparation slack himself. She may similarly recognize that he is out of sorts after competing for precedence in a male-dominated hierarchy and allow him to unwind by watching mindless television. Under these conditions, it may subsequently be easier for each to make the concessions necessary to achieve bargains that address the needs of both.

This newly emerging flexibility as to the household division of labor has reduced the time women spend on housework, but is has not completely equalized who does what. This is particularly true once children arrive. However modern a couple, the birth of their first child usually pushes them toward more traditional arrangements. She becomes more concerned with raising their offspring and he more dedicated to providing for their financial security. Should she, for instance, decide that she does not enjoy motherhood, she will find that her friends and relatives disapprove of her choice. Like it or not, to be regarded as a poor mother is tantamount to be judged a failure as a woman. Similarly, should he claim the Mr. Mom role, his friends and relatives will almost surely lose respect for him as a man. In due course, even his wife—although she has previously urged him to stay home and care for their brood—will grow impatient. Why, she will wonder, does she need to put up with this hanger-on when she can afford to hire a less demanding housekeeper?

The distressing truth is that dramatic role reversals frequently precipitate divorce. When she works and he doesn't, this is apt to precipitate a separation within a half-dozen years. Likewise, if she makes significantly more money than he does, he will probably feel his manhood threatened, whereas she will lose respect for a man she views as less powerful than herself. Because the husband is still regarded as the primary breadwinner, especially when there are children involved, a couple is more likely to move to enhance his job prospects rather than hers. This may not be fair, but it is in accord with what continues to be a broad social consensus on gender-based roles.

Needless to say the nature of the marital relationship will be modified as the children grow older and as the economic circumstances of the family shift. The tasks that must be accomplished when raising toddlers are not the same as those appropriate for teenagers. Even more significant alterations occur when the children move out and a couple is left on their own. Women frequently become more vocationally successful at this point. No longer diverted by family responsibilities, they redirect their energies toward the workplace. This, in turn, may alter her relationship with her spouse. In other words, individual and mutual growth, and therefore continued interpersonal negotiations, are a persistent feature of the successful marriage.

DIVORCE

Then again, not all marriages are successful. Today a great many of them end in divorce. Conventional wisdom has it that about half of all contemporary marriages end in divorce, and this is pretty much the case. What is misleading is the implication that half of all first marriages do so, which is not the situation. Only about a third of these do. The reason for this disparity is that some people get divorced two, three, or more times. Moreover, second, third, and fourth marriages are more vulnerable to divorce than are first marriages. Many people do not learn from failed marriages and continue to make similar mistakes. The good news is that divorce does seem to be on the decline. People appear to be learning that the hasty dissolution of an unhappy alliance is not a sure-fire cure for personal distress.

The largest number of divorces take place at about the fourth year of a union. After that the proportion continues to decline into old age. Why divorces occur, however, is not completely understood. The usual excuses, namely fights over money and sex, are just that—excuses. Couples do argue about these things, but they are indicators of underlying tensions, not their cause. After all, many poor people have strong marriages and sexual issues can be resolved. Years ago, sexual therapists flourished, but they are now less prominent. The reason is that the single most significant source of sexual dysfunction is that parties to a marriage do not like each other. It is difficult to be aroused by someone perceived as an enemy.

But why does one perceive an intimate as an enemy? Why would someone once regarded as a savior mutate into an implacable foe? Social scientists have become quite skilled at determining when frictions are liable to escalate toward divorce. It is clear that when a husband or wife undercut one another in public, this is an excellent sign they are headed toward a separation. But investigators have been less able to determine what drives them apart in the first place. Why, when they once seemed able to meet each other's needs, do they arrive at an impasse where they do the opposite?

A hint at what is occurring comes from a well-established finding. Early marriage is strongly correlated with divorce. The younger a couple is when they make a commitment, the more fragile this pledge is apt to be. Most teenagers do not yet understand what sort of person they are likely to become, and they are not accurately able to identify the sort of person a potential partner will be. No wonder that after a number of years they discover that this other person is headed on a different trajectory. Under these conditions they grow apart and find they are no longer able to accommodate each other's needs.

Growing apart may also occur under other circumstances. One partner, for instance, may continue to mature after marriage, while the other adopts a defensive stance and refuses to make personal adjustments. In the best scenario, a husband and wife assist each other in overcoming difficulties emanating from their respective childhoods. They talk about their pasts and provide emotional solace when each confronts a personal bugaboo. When this occurs, they can move toward greater maturity in tandem. When it does not, one partner may become a full adult, while the other remains mired in a rigid self-protective posture. In this latter case, it may ultimately become impossible for them to negotiate their differences. They may even have difficulty in sustaining a civil conversation.

Be this as it may, sociologists have developed an excellent understanding of the various stages of divorce. These more or less follow the same sequence as occurs in the case of death. Elizabeth Kubler-Ross in studying death and dying discovered that people traverse a predictable course in coming to terms with a severe loss. They begin in a state of denial. When, let us say, an older woman sends her husband of many years out to the supermarket where he sustains a fatal heart attack, the stranger who comes to her door to inform her of this tragedy is liable not to be believed. News this bad is unconsciously rejected. It is so forcefully denied that even after the woman understands that her husband is gone, when she hears footfalls outside her door, her first reaction will be that these must be his.

The second step of the grieving process is apt to be anger. Our bereaved wife may now grow angry at her departed spouse. How, she will wonder, could he have left her? How could he, who promised to be with her forever, have deserted her so completely? When now forced to pay the bills that he once managed, she will gnash her teeth at his failure to come to her rescue. Intermingled with this resentment will also be a bargaining process. In our society, the conventional format for this sort of negotiation is an attempt to make a deal with God. Thus she may silently pray to wake up and find that this is all a bad dream. If the Deity will just let her know that this was a terrible mistake, she will promise to go to church each Sunday without fail.

It is only after these attempts to reverse a significant loss that a person grows sad. This is the crucial stage of the mourning process. It is the point at which a person begins to sever his or her attachments to what is gone. After protests against the loss have fallen short, the mourner enters a deep depression. During this period he or she detaches from normal life and becomes despondent. The person turns inward and loses his or her motivation to engage in customary activities. There may be episodes of tears; there will surely be a mental review of incidents from the past. In this, the individual is essentially breaking the bonds that have developed during the relationship. The person, in sequence, is forced to recognize that this is gone, and that that is gone, and so is this other.

It is only subsequent to this that a person is able to move on. Acceptance of a significant loss takes time. The emotional reorganization necessary for an uncomplicated death usually lasts about a year. This is why our society provides mourners with an interval when fewer demands are made of them. When complications arise—as with the unexpected death of a young child—letting go can take longer, sometimes many years. In the case of divorce, which it must be recognized is also a loss, the average length of mourning is about three years. Since this loss is more ambiguous than is death, lingering hopes for a reconciliation can keep the parties from completing the process.

To reiterate, divorce is a serious loss. It is not something that married couples welcome. Even with marital dissolution as common as it has become, people enter the institution on the assumption that their union will last forever. They do not go into it assuming that five good years will be sufficient. For most, divorce comes as a surprise. The relationship may have become rocky, but the partners will dismiss their quarrels as a standard part of being married. In essence, due to denial, it may take a series of disasters before one or both decide that their union cannot be salvaged. Often one party comes to this conclusion before the other; hence when the latter is asked for a divorce, it comes as a bolt from the blue.

No wonder that when anger finally intercedes, it can be violent. For understandable reasons, each party feels betrayed by the other. What had been taken to be a solemn commitment is now being cast aside without apparent regard for the other's feelings. Each may, as a result, think, "I have given you the best years of my life and this is how you repay me?" So furious can the parties become that their strongest desire is for revenge. Movies such as *The War between the Tates* capture just how passionate the ensuing pyrotechnics can become. The goal is not to let go, but to inflict a commensurate injury.

In divorce, bargaining occurs in two primary guises. The first is an attempt at reconciliation. The warring spouses may agree to see a marital counselor in an effort to resolve their disputes. The two may believe all that is needed is improved communication skills. Unhappily, they are apt to discover that in clarifying their messages they have grown to hate each other. Thus, in many cases, family therapy entered into as a means of maintaining a marriage becomes a vestibule to its termination. Instead of producing acceptable agreements, it demonstrates that these are no longer possible.

Lawyers may mediate the second sort of bargaining. These negotiations concentrate on how to divide up the marital assets. Who will get the house, the silverware, or the children? But because the parties have long since ceased feeling friendly toward one another, they are unlikely to feel generous. The major concern is now with making sure that one is not cheated by this other person—this scoundrel who has become an irredeemable villain. Even the smallest items become major bones of contention when the underlying goal is to get revenge.

When divorce was still unusual, when people had to travel out to Reno to obtain final papers, its was often assumed that the final decree would occasion a celebration. It was expected that the parties would be thrilled to achieve their freedom. Yet this is not generally what occurs. Divorce, let it be said once more, is a loss. It is a failure. It is a dream that has crashed and burned. This is not a happy moment. It is rather one of deep sadness. Even when the marriage was a disaster, even when the other person truly was an abusive villain, divorce hurts. At the very least, it represents the death of a fond hope. That which was deeply desired, even if it were never possible, is now gone beyond retrieval. This surely is, and must be, depressing.

Furthermore, it must be remembered that the infatuation stage of courtship established an emotional attachment that is now being torn asunder. A person who had been built into one's life must now be ushered out of it. This is what sadness is intended to accomplish. It is the central mechanism for cutting ties with what is gone. It must therefore be experienced if a person is to move on. This is why those undergoing divorce spend many hours ruminating about what went wrong. They are engaged in a step-by-step process of relinquishing that which cannot be salvaged. Should they not do so, they would be trapped in an unremittingly painful past.

If those undergoing divorce too quickly reenter the dating scene, they discover that they are not prepared for a new relationship. When they sit down to dinner with a new person, they find themselves enmeshed in the old liaison. The topic of discussion is almost invariably the former partner. This, of course, is not the best way to establish a fresh start. It may take time before a person has sufficiently accepted what has gone wrong to begin looking forward. Only then will a new someone be seen for who he or she truly is. Only then can the lessons available from the previous fiasco be assimilated so as to prevent its repetition.

DIVORCE AND CHILDREN

So far almost nothing has been said about the children that may result from a marriage. How are they affected by divorce? When the concept of divorce was still novel, conventional wisdom had it that children were resilient. No matter how painful the blow, it was expected that they would recover. Indeed, divorce was alleged to be beneficial for the young. If a marriage were a disaster, liberating them from this would free them from a poisonous relationship that was bound to injure them too. Mothers, in particular, were advised that in emancipating themselves from a brutish male, they were setting a good example for their children. In pursuing personal autonomy, they were demonstrating the utility of self-esteem. They were essentially giving their offspring permission to be their own persons and to protect themselves from interpersonal bondage.

The problem with this scenario is that it was stated from the parent's point of view, not the child's. Children suffer from divorce. They are its collateral damage. As already mentioned, their life prospects go into a tailspin after divorce. Their lifestyle also declines when their father departs and leaves their mother in diminished economic circumstances. They thus become victims of what has been called the feminization of poverty. Their educational attainments also decline when they lose the will to study and when the resources to send then to college vanish. Likewise, their marital prospects wane as they become depressed and lose faith in the dependability of members of the opposite sex.

But to begin at the beginning, children suffer most because they almost never want their parents to divorce. From their perspective, their parents have always been together. They are perceived as a couple, rather than as individuals with separate histories. So powerful is this perception that one of enduring aspirations of the children of divorce is that their parents will eventually reconcile. Movies such as the various versions of *The Parent Trap* are extremely popular because they present a warm-hearted depiction of parents discovering that separation was a mistake. In the end, they come to their senses and prove that marriage truly is forever.

Because divorce represents a loss for children as well as their parents, the young too must undergo a period of mourning if they are to adjust to this crisis. Unfortunately, as children they do not exercise much control over this process. They are at the mercy of their parents—parents who generally do not want their children to experience grief. First, most parents do not want to see their children in such pain. But second, and more important, this pain would be a reproach to their own selfishness. It would imply that the parents' desire for happiness is causing their offspring's suffering. As distressed and confused as these adults probably are, they do not need the additional overload of a child's anguished pleas. The result is that they typically demand that their children suppress their misery.

Children too begin by denying the divorce. They usually cannot bring themselves to recognize that their parents are separating; hence they ignore what is occurring. But then they get angry. They may now demand that mommy and daddy not do this. Whereas their parents were probably quite content with the earlier denials, they will be equally distressed by this emerging antagonism. Children are not supposed to be angry with their parents. They may therefore be told, in one way or another, to shut up. The parents may also attempt to strengthen their children's denials by explaining that everything will be okay. Daddy is not really leaving; mommy is not really upset, etc., etc.

Once it becomes clear that daddy truly is leaving, junior may tug at his trousers attempting to bargain this development out of existence. On the mistaken assumption that he is responsible for this catastrophe, he will promise to be good if only daddy will stay. When daddy goes, however, there will be sadness, or rather there would be sadness, if it were permitted. If parents perceive anger as a reproach, sadness is doubly viewed as such. It screams out loud that mommy and daddy are inflicting pain on the child. Thus it is flat out disallowed. Children will be cajoled and bullied into pretending that they are coping just fine. In other words, they will not be permitted to experience the sadness that is necessary to let go. They will be forced to repress it with the consequence that they are not able to work through their loss.

But what is repressed is not gone. It lingers in the unconscious awaiting an opportunity to return to the surface where it can finally be resolved. This is why the children of divorce frequently experience wild gyrations once they come of age. It is why they often settle on unsuitable partners when making their own way into adulthood. What they are attempting to do is to recapitulate the circumstances of the divorce so that they can at long last mourn it. They desperately want to let go, but are handicapped in doing so because what they are attempting to achieve may not be clear, even to them.

Other problems issuing from divorce surround what have been called blended, or reconstituted, families. Not surprisingly, divorced parents frequently seek to remarry. A woman may begin dating other men in the hope of finding love and perhaps a substitute father for her child. What she unexpectedly encounters from her child is resentment. From the child's point of view, a new relationship would be a nail in the coffin of the old one. It would definitely prevent the longed for reconciliation between the parents. Thus when asked to be friendly toward this stranger, the child's reaction is anger. Also confusing is the likelihood that a child will be friendlier toward an absent parent than the custodial one. She will generally blame her mother for the divorce rather than the daddy who takes her out on alternate weekends. This, paradoxically, is a sign that she trusts the caretaker parent more. Her evident loyalty makes it safer to be irate with her.

Nor need all of these currents and countercurrents subside in the wake of remarriage. The Brady Bunch was decidedly fiction. Two families gathering together under a single roof does not automatically make for one blissfully happy extended clan. For starters, new parents are rarely accepted as legitimate sources of authority. The eternal complaint of the child disciplined by a stepparent is, "You're not my father (or mother)." Nor do siblings from different parents necessarily get along. Both sides may be fearful of favoritism directed toward stepsiblings. They will suspect that a stepparent naturally supports his (or her) biological kin.

These problems can be overcome, but this requires time and patience. Anger and suspicion do not dissipate merely because they are unpleasant. People do not stop feeling these things because this would be the rational response. Negative feelings must be worked through. If mourning is necessary, mourning must occur. If the trustworthiness of new relatives needs to be tested, it must be tested. And these others must pass the test. Yet all of this may require super-maturity on the part of those concerned.

Questions

1. Is marriage obsolete? Are there alternatives to marriage? What might these be?
2. What other advantages might marriage have than those enumerated in this chapter? What disadvantages does it harbor?
3. Have you experienced any of the stages of courtship? What was your reaction when in the midst of them?
4. Should marriage be fifty-fifty? Should men be prepared to move to a different state to facilitate a wife's new job?
5. Should a couple postpone divorce for the sake of the children? Will this help or hurt?

Selected Readings

Cherlin, A. J. 1992. *Marriage, Divorce, and Remarriage.* Cambridge, MA: Harvard University Press.

Fisher, H. E. 1992. *Anatomy of Love: The Natural History of Monogamy, Adultery and Divorce.* New York: W. W. Norton & Co.

Waite, C. J., and Gallagher, M. 2000. *The Case for Marriage: Why Married People Are Happier, Healthier, and Better Off Financially.* New York: Doubleday.

Wallenstein, J. S., Lewis, J. M., and Blakesee, S. 2000. *The Unexpected Legacy of Divorce: A 25-Year Landmark Study.* New York: Hyperion.

Getting Down to Business: Bureaucracy and Professionalism

COMMAND AND CONTROL

The Romans were arrogant. They had conquered Britain and they were determined to make the most of it. The local tribes were to be treated as supplicants, who, if they objected, would be coerced back into submission. One of these tribes was the Iceni. After several clashes, the Romans murdered their king, and then raped his wife and daughters. What they had not calculated on was the grit of the Iceni queen. Boadicea by name (nowadays frequently spelled *Boudica*), she incited her tribe and several surrounding tribes to rebellion. Within short order, over a hundred thousand Britons descended upon the towns that became Colchester and London, burning and pillaging as they went. Terror spread in their wake and it seemed as if the imperialistic Roman machine were about to be annihilated.

Meanwhile the Roman governor Caius Suetonius Paulinus was up north in Wales putting down the Druid opposition there. Upon hearing the news, he headed south with an army of about ten thousand. Along the way he met the British host moving to intercept him. But he did not chance upon this horde in an accidental fashion. Informed of the movements of his foe, he carefully chose a battlefield that would favor him. This was a broad grassland area bordered by forests that converged in a V-shape. He stationed his men where the woodlands came together so that the larger British force would be compressed into a narrow front as it surged forward to attack. This, he knew, would help equal the more than ten-to-one odds.

Boadicea, for her part, was confident. She and her warriors were fresh from slaughtering thousands of Romans and they knew they greatly outnumbered their enemy. Moreover, they were ferocious fighters. Festooned in blue paint, and wielding huge broadswords, they were accustomed to running headlong into an opponent's lines and terrifying them with their sheer intensity. The mere sight of tens of thousands of wild men waving their weapons over their heads was usually sufficient to set their adversaries into flight. Boadicea expected nothing less

103

this time. Consequently, her strategy consisted solely in setting her multitudes into action—backed up by a wagon train carrying their supplies and families.

What she had not counted on was that Paulinus commanded a very different sort of army. His was far more disciplined. The Roman military was organized into legions and cohorts under the iron command of generals and centurions. The soldiers themselves were armed with pillions and the gladius. They threw their spears on command and stood shoulder to shoulder in the face of the most aggressive foe. This enabled them to overlap their shields so that the enemy's weapons could not penetrate. They were also able to replace those on the front line at a signal from their leaders. This made sure that those up front had the energy to continue the fight. They would then take their short swords and thrust them upward into the exposed bellies of their opponents. Only when this stopped the foe in his tracks would they, again at a signal from above, move forward in a wedge-shaped formation that trapped the fleeing enemy between relentless echelons.

When this apparatus was set in motion against the Britons the effects were devastating. The each-man-for-himself natives were no match for such well-practiced discipline. Once on the attack, they had no way to stop even when things went wrong. Moreover, once in flight they had no means of reorganizing their ranks. As a result, they were cut down from behind in the tens of thousands. The slaughter became even worse when they ran into their own wagon train and could not escape the Roman wrath. Boadicea could do nothing to reverse this massacre. As brave, determined, and powerful as she was, she had no method of regaining control of her forces. They were a tribal mob, not a regimented military.

The point of this example is to demonstrate the utility of what soldiers call command and control. That which enables a large group of people to engage in a coordinated activity is often a centralized management with the clout to enforce its directives. This sort of social structure permits a comprehensive design to be imposed from on top. Grounded in hierarchical and social role principles, it allows for consistency and harmonization of action. Different individuals, with different motives and mind-sets, are thereby brought together for a common objective. They are subordinated to a single purpose such that they become far more powerful than a disorganized horde.

We today are accustomed to this sort of coordination because we are familiar with participating in complex organizations. What most of us do not realize is how recent this form of supervision is. We work in large corporations governed by bureaucratic principles and we imagine that this has always been so. Yes, the Roman military possessed a rudimentary bureaucracy, and so did the early Roman Catholic Church, but not until the Industrial Revolution did most economic entities do so. In the Middle Ages, for instance, cooperation depended more on personal relations than on impersonal associations. Whom you knew, whom you liked, and whom you were related to mattered more than your place in a systematic form of supervision.

Family ties helped establish even national borders during the feudal epoch. Getting married to the right person could double the size of a political entity in an instant. Such was the good fortune of Henry II of England when he wed Eleanor of Aquitaine. Suddenly he controlled more territory in France than did his nominal overlord Louis VII. He could even challenge the authority of this man to whom he theoretically owed allegiance. The tables were turned, however, during the reign of Louis's son Philip II (also called Philip Augustus). Philip forged an alliance with Henry's son Richard, known to history as the Lion-Heart. Richard distrusted his father's intentions, so he was happy to collaborate in his demise. Together with

Philip, he helped defeat Henry, which in time led to the loss of Aquitaine, and eventually under his brother John to the loss of most of northern France as well.

Today the manager of a Ford assembly plant could hardly switch his alliance to General Motors, thereby enhancing the power of the latter. Although he could quit one company and be hired by the other, he could not take the factory he managed with him. In the Middle Ages things were different. People did not so much belong to organizations as maintain alliances with particular individuals. If these alliances shifted, then so did the boundaries of who controlled what. Occupational positions as we know them today had not yet developed; hence military power and personal loyalties typically determined areas of authority.

The invention, or rather the proliferation, of bureaucracy changed all this. Bureaucracies are much more precise. They more clearly define who is in charge of whom and what sorts of activities each will perform. As a result, they can organize far more complex functions. They can hold a company as large as General Motors together, whereas feudal arrangements decidedly could not. As the sociologist Max Weber has explained, bureaucracy has made our modern mass-market society possible. It is the glue that permits large-scale associations to operate. Without it, the prosperity we take for granted, and the nation-states to which we pledge allegiance, would not even be figments of the imagination.

BUREAUCRACY

Few people love bureaucracy. Most of us, at one time or another, curse it under our breath. We berate the stupid red tape and bemoan the lack of freedom. And yet, most of us, at one point or another, will work for a bureaucracy. We will take a job with a large company or with the federal government and will have to follow its rules. Even if we don't, we will inevitably do business with bureaucracies. We will purchase their products or be subject to regulations they enforce. It is thus incumbent upon us to understand what makes bureaucracies tick. How are they put together and how does this affect the way they do business?

In some respects bureaucracies can be incredibly inefficient. They can be rigid and mean-spirited. Nevertheless there is commonly no alternative to them. If an enterprise requires large-scale control and command, nothing else will do. So how are they configured? What is special about the way they are put together? Weber's analysis remains pertinent. He has described six critical aspects of their operation. The first has to do with their objectives. According to him, a bureaucracy must have overarching organizational goals. If it is to constitute a single entity, it must possess a unifying sense of direction. Although the participants will have personal goals, while they are doing the organization's business they must subordinate these to its larger purposes. If they work for General Motors, they must share a commitment to producing automobiles. If they are employed by the Internal Revenue Service, they must be prepared to collect taxes. To reject these goals is to refuse to participate in the organization.

Nowadays organizational goals are frequently framed as mission statements. They are literally put into words so that members of the organization understand what is required, while those who do business with the establishment will know what to expect. These statements are frequently more about public relations than accurately encapsulating what is done, but they nevertheless make a difference. They at least express an idealization of that to which the players are committed.

The second universal feature of bureaucracies is a *functional division of labor.* These divide complex jobs into a set of interlocking tasks. Instead of expecting one person to complete every operation necessary to achieve a goal, these are separated so that those assigned them can become expert in their performance. This sort of specialization increases efficiencies dramatically. Adam Smith long ago provided the most famous example of what can be accomplished. As the father of modern economic thinking, he used a pin factory to illustrate what was possible. In the past, said Smith, when individual blacksmiths fabricated pins, they began with the metal, formed it into wires, cut these in pieces, and finally added sharp points and heads. In this way, they could produce several dozen pins a day.

But, continued Smith, when separate individuals were assigned to prepare the metal, form it into wires, cut these into pieces, and so forth, productivity shot up. Together they could generate many hundreds of pins per day. No longer having to jump from task to task, they could concentrate on their individual contributions. This same premise underlies the contemporary factory. These industrial operations do not merely bring hundreds of people together under the same roof; they also assign them distinct aspects of a larger process. This way they are more effective than they would be in isolation.

The third universal feature that bureaucracies exhibit concerns how this functional division of labor is applied. Individuals are not assigned separate tasks willy-nilly. These are distributed into *defined offices.* Each person has a designated set of responsibilities that he or she is expected to perform. Today we have a word for these specified collections of tasks; we call them *jobs.* What jobs do is to convert a set of duties into a social role. This collection of activities is so closely associated with the individual who performs them that they can come to constitute part of his or her identity. So familiar is this concept that we think it has been around forever. Now, while it is true that distinct occupations have been around for a long time, assigning them to particular individuals within an organizational setting has not. During the Middle Ages, for example, serfs might be expected to do a little of this and a little of that. They simply did what ever was needed when it was needed, as did their overlords. None of them were restricted to a cluster of duties listed in a job description.

The invention of defined offices changed this. In creating organizational specializations, it fostered the development of expertise. People could now be hired based on their abilities to perform specific operations. They could also be paid on the basis of how well they executed their separate roles. This supplied both the incentive and the ability to do these well. A person with excellent fine motor dexterity could be hired as a typist and promoted if she handled this post efficiently. By the same token, someone with first-rate mechanical aptitude could be employed as a machinist, where he would later be remunerated commensurate with his output.

The next universal feature of bureaucracies is their dependence on a *hierarchy of authority.* Hierarchies go back to hunter-gatherer times, but as organizations grew larger face-to-face tests of personal strength became less possible. What was needed was a more reliable, less contentious means of assigning authority to some people over others. Bureaucracies achieve this through chains of command. These as clearly stipulate who is to give orders to whom as they specify defined offices. When hired into a bureaucracy a person will be instructed as to who is his or her boss, as well as which persons are his or her subordinates. More than this, the individual will learn the areas of authority each of these commands. He or she will understand that a boss can tell a subordinate how to perform a particular job, but not which movie to see on the weekend. One is within his mandate whereas the other is not.

This clarity as to who is in charge and exactly what they are in charge of facilitates command and control. It allows orders to pass down through the sequence of authority such that what the top boss orders will be carried out by the multitude of lower-ranking workers at the bottom of the pyramid. Speed of operation as well as accuracy in spelling out directions are thereby facilitated. Bureaucracies can turn on a dime compared with barbarian hordes. General Motors can go from painting automobiles blue to coating them in red the very next day. A comprehensive hierarchy of authority also promotes continuity of command. Even though the individuals who occupy particular posts may change, as long as the areas of command they represent remain constant, the organization can persist as a recognizable entity. There may be a new president at General Motors, but he will still be president of the same company.

Bureaucracies are also rife with *rules and procedures*. Those who are attached to them are not only constrained as to organizational goals, defined offices, and specific spans of authority, they are also instructed on how they are supposed to perform their various duties. Because the central objective is the efficient attainment of the organizational goals, rational modes of realizing these are theoretically built into detailed regulations. The organization specifies the correct way to do things and the participants are expected to follow suit. Just as competence is to be derived from intelligently dividing tasks and then assigning them to the most appropriate workers, so is it to flow from promoting the most suitable methods of operation.

Unfortunately, it is not always clear which are the most efficient modes of operation. Efficiency experts committed to scientific management believe they can figure out the optimum procedures, but not everyone is so sure. Herbert Simon argues that the best one can do is to *satisfice*, that is, to find a satisfactory solution. Nevertheless, if one makes a mistake, one should fix it. In any event, strictly formulated rules tend to degenerate into red tape. They are liable to be regarded as ends in themselves even when an objective evaluation would conclude they are neither effective nor appropriate. Red tape is notorious for its rigidity and foolish consistency—for its this-is-the-way-it's-done attitude irrespective of the consequences.

Last, bureaucracies are dependent upon *files and records.* Once an organization grows past a certain size, it can no longer rely on human memory. There will simply be too many items for workers to keep in mind. It will also be impossible to provide continuity if critical information is lost whenever key individuals leave. Files and records are essentially the memory of the organization. Writing things down (or filing them on a computer) provides objective documentation of what has transpired and/or what has been promised. It enables commercial companies to keep track of orders and deliveries, while universities can maintain evidence of a student's grades no matter how many years have elapsed. Files and records are especially critical when money is involved. Not only do they prevent cheating, but they also make it possible to calculate what is profitable and what is not.

The problem here is that files and records, like rules and procedures, can become ends in themselves. Occupants of the bureaucracy can lose sight of the organizational goals if they get too tied up in their day-to-day clerical duties. They become victims of goal displacement, with what they record becoming more important than why they record it in the first place. They may, for instance, regard easily obtained statistics as a higher priority than attaining their original purpose. Like baseball players fixated on inflating their batting averages, they forget that what really matters is winning the game. In this case, they can become like the ritualists of which Merton spoke.

In summing this up, Weber suggested that the motto of bureaucracy should be *sine ira et studio*. Derived from Latin, this phrase is generally translated as "without fear or favor." Bureaucracy, as opposed to its organizational predecessors, is less dependent on coercion. Under feudalism, for instance, a recalcitrant serf could be cut down without penalty by an impatient baron. So might a slave who disobeyed his master. In the modern corporation, in contrast, people get demoted, or at worst fired. They do what they do not because they are physically threatened if they don't, but because they have agreed to serve in roles that are rewarded for the desired performance.

Nor are defined offices or positions of authority supposed to be distributed according to personal relationships. Who gets hired or promoted is not expected to hinge on who is friends or relatives with whom. Favoritism is frowned upon. So is nepotism. Niches within the bureaucracy are purportedly dependent upon skill and ability. The most competent person, not the best liked, is supposed to be selected. To be sure, this objective is frequently honored in the breach. Too often success depends on whom you know not what you know, but this happenstance is regarded as illegitimate. We make jokes about the boss's son moving up the corporate ladder or about his wife sitting on the board of directors. Many people even resented it when President Kennedy appointed his brother Robert to the position of attorney general.

Weber, when reviewing how bureaucracies elicited compliance, was struck by how successful they were. Their employees habitually followed the rules without overtly rebelling. He called this phenomenon the "iron cage." Workers "went along to get along." They didn't "rock the boat" not because they feared being whipped, but because they didn't want to get fired. They voluntarily accepted submission within this large social structure because they could see no alternative to doing so. They might not enjoy having to obey orders or follow procedures, but in a market economy in a *Gesellschaft* world there was no other choice.

POWER AND AUTHORITY

Nowadays we like to think of ourselves as living in a civilized society. We flatter ourselves by believing that the way we do things is rationally organized. Certainly that is the way Weber viewed bureaucracy. Ideally it was supposed to institutionalize the most effective means of achieving desired ends. But most of us know this is not exactly so. We understand that people compete for power for power's sake, and that some people come out as winners whereas others emerge as losers. This may not be nice, but we recognize that it is the way of the social world.

Weber's analysis of the way power works is useful here too. He defined power as the ability to get people to do things even if they do not want to. Despite their resistance or apathy, they follow the directions of the more powerful individual. They do so for several reasons. They might, for instance, be coerced into submission. In this case, they would be forced to do what they initially did not wish to do. For the most part, this is accomplished not by physically manipulating people, but by frightening them into compliance. Small children may be pulled into the dining room despite wanting to watch TV, whereas adults are threatened with negative consequences. They are not so much punished as promised that they will be punished if they do not obey. Thus their bosses never physically throw them out on the street, but rather intimate that they might be fired for insubordination.

Of equal importance in obtaining compliance is promising a reward. People will do what they had not intended if they believe there may be a positive payoff for doing so. They join bureaucracies not merely for an opportunity to participate in fulfilling their goals, but because they expect to get paid. Similarly, they perform overtime for extra compensation or they turn in quality work because they hope this will produce a promotion at a higher salary. People will even do what they are asked for a reward as modest as a warm smile. Some psychologists have argued that reward is a much better motivator than is punishment, but the sad truth seems to be that a combination of both succeeds better than either in isolation. In other words, carrots and sticks in combination are more effective than either alone.

Another manifestation of power, however, is authority. Authority is present when people voluntarily comply with what is required. Authority is legitimate power. It is lawful and valid power. Long ago Chester Barnard pointed out that power is frequently projected on leaders. They may not literally possess the ability to coerce or reward their subordinates, but if they are thought to, this may be sufficient. The mere habit of others in complying with what they desire confers influence on them. Whatever a leader's personal qualities or resources, if his or her underlings are prepared to obey, it is as if he or she could compel them to do so.

Weber distinguished between three types of authority. The first is traditional authority. This is power that is conferred on someone because this is the way things have always been done. It is the sort of authority that belongs to a monarch in a nation that has long been ruled by a king. Under these conditions, the mere thought of defying a ruler's decrees seems unimaginable.

The feeling of a monarch's subjects is much the same as that of an adult male who is asked to beat his mother. Although he as grown larger and stronger than she, the idea of laying a hand on her, even if she does something untoward, is inconceivable. One does not hit one's mother—no matter what. Nor does one willfully flout her wishes. Mothers deserve respect. We are conditioned to obeying them. Once upon a time, when we were small, our mothers could coerce us into doing what they desired. But this vulnerable feeling outlasts their ability to impose their will. It is eventually built into our emotional memories; hence even as adults the idea of defying them sends shivers down our spines. We may not consciously know why, but we do as we are told. Yet in so doing, we participate in maintaining their authority.

The second type of authority is charismatic. Some people just seem to have the sort of personality that elicits compliance. We want to do what they ask because there is something special about them. They seem surrounded by a magical aura. John Kennedy had charisma. Martin Luther King had charisma. But George W. Bush does not. Bush may be a good man, but he is not a particularly inspirational one. He is not a Ronald Reagan or a Franklin Delano Roosevelt. But then again, Harry Truman did not have charisma either. Charisma and competence are not necessarily joined at the hip.

Charisma need not even attach to a good person. Adolf Hitler had charisma. So did Vladimir Lenin and Mao Tse-tung. What charismatic people seem to have in common is an ability to make others believe that they are concerned about their personal welfare. When they listen to others, charismatic leaders do so in such a concentrated manner that the recipient of their attentions is made to feel special. Or if they give a speech, as Hitler often did, they do so with such emotional intensity that their listeners feel as if the message is directed specifically toward them. Charisma confers authority because people want to repay what they feel is being given to them by the charismatic person.

The last Weberian mode of authority is the rational-legal. This type of authority derives from a person's position within a bureaucracy. When someone is delegated authority within this sort of organization, the power to give orders comes from the legitimacy of the organization itself. If the organization is believed rational in its pursuit of desired goals, then those who give instructions in accord with its defined offices, chain of command, and rules and procedures are liable to have their directives respected. Irrespective of their personal qualities, or their individual ability to confer rewards or punishments, they share in the potency of the organization. Others know that if these persons give lawful orders, their bureaucratic superiors will back them up.

Consider a professor who requires his students to take an examination. He may be an incompetent teacher and they may hate the idea of studying for a test, but they quietly do as they are told. As a group, they could easily defy him. They could literally rise up to tie and bind him to his chair. But they don't. They understand that because the organization gives him the right to impose examinations, the dean and college president will stand by him. They also understand that their defiance might lead to their dismissal from the university. Were the professor, however, to demand that they dye their hair red, the situation would be otherwise. This order would be neither rational nor legal; hence it would lack authority. The professor would no longer be able to count on his allies within the organization, with the consequence that his legitimacy would vanish.

It might be thought that rational-legal authority comes automatically with one's appointment to a position of bureaucratic power, but this is not quite true. When people are promoted within organizations they must demonstrate that they possess the personal qualities commensurate with their new status. They must prove to their new subordinates that they possess the personal strength to exercise power. It should not be forgotten that hierarchical positions are ultimately grounded in tests of strength. This means that workers will frequently disobey a new leader in order to discover if he or she possesses the ability to force their compliance. It also means that a new leader may create an opportunity to impose his or her will. In organizations, they say that, "A new broom sweeps clean." This is but a colorful way of communicating that newly appointed managers tend to reorganize their bailiwicks in order to assert their authority.

Such an incident occurred in an episode of *Star Trek—The Next Generation*. Regular viewers of this series will appreciate that Jean-Luc Picard was an excellent leader. As captain he had the respect of his crew and exercised a firmly established authority. Nevertheless, he was at one point reassigned to a special mission. While he was gone, another captain was appointed in his place. This new officer began by directing his second in command, the redoubtable Commander James Riker, to reorganize how the *Enterprise's* shifts were arranged. The next day he asked Riker if these changes had been implemented. When Riker responded that they had not, that the old arrangements under Picard had worked just fine, the new captain was outraged. He told Riker in no uncertain terms that if he did not do as he was ordered, he would be relieved of command. Most viewers were undoubtedly dismayed by this heavy-handedness. They respected Riker. Riker was their hero. How could he possibly be chastised so cavalierly?

The answer, of course, was that the new captain had to prove a point. He needed to make it crystal clear to everyone aboard that he was now in charge. This was especially so if he were to follow in the shoes of as respected a leader as Picard. If the new captain could demonstrate that he was more powerful than Riker, who was himself the second most powerful person aboard the ship, he would thereby demonstrate that he was now the most powerful. In effortlessly threatening to fire Riker, he demonstrated that he was not to be trifled with. Had he backed down, had Riker instead intimidated him, the opposite lesson would have been communicated. In this case, members of the crew would have lost respect for him and despite his position would have been more likely to do what Riker asked. Rational-legal authority, in short, must be backed by personal potency if it is to be effectively leveraged.

PROFESSIONALISM

Ever since Weber codified our understanding of how bureaucracies operate, it has been conventional wisdom that bureaucracies are taking over society. Some have thought that we are becoming "McDonaldized." They believe that most jobs are being reduced to the level of those at McDonalds. Hamburger flippers at fast food restaurants are certainly consigned to clearly defined jobs circumscribed by a host of simple procedures. They have very little discretion in performing relatively boring jobs. For them, the iron cage has become a plastic detention center. They can look out and see others enjoying the fruits of their labors, but they cannot escape the drudgery of their tasks.

The McDonalization thesis asserts that more and more jobs are becoming similarly deskilled. As bureaucracy proliferates, tasks are presumably more finely divided and procedures ever more detailed. Growing demands for uniformity and precision take the humanity out of a majority of employments and reduce people to mindless cogs in organizational machines. People may hate laboring on assembly lines where they constantly turn the same sorts of nuts on the same sorts of bolts, but they take what is available. If what they do during the day is not rewarding, they instead seek fulfillment in their avocations rather than their vocations.

In fact, there is a viable alternative to routinized bureaucratization. It is called professionalism. Where bureaucracy is centralized, professionalism is decentralized. Where bureaucracy is lashed to shared regulations and impersonal procedures, professionalism relies on personal competence and individual dedication. Professions have been around almost as long as bureaucracies, but they have until recently been confined to a relatively few occupations. Historically, there were three professional groups: the doctors, the lawyers, and the ministers. Each of these did work that was considered so vital that those engaged in their service were deemed to have been called by God. Theirs was literally a "calling." It was a "profession" in the sense that what they professed was in accord with the wishes of the deity. To be a professional was thus to be dedicated to the benefit of humanity.

The best way to understand what makes the professions special is to analyze what it takes to be a physician. To begin with, physicians have special knowledge. They understand how the human body functions and are familiar with the effects that various medications have on it. In short, doctors know how to cure illnesses to a degree that laypersons don't. Moreover, this knowledge is difficult to master. It is not as if ordinary people could acquire it by perusing the *Reader's Digest*. Physicians also get credit for participating in the creation of this knowledge. Their involvement in fundamental research helps to uncover the facts that they later apply to medical practice.

Because they are stewards of exclusive and valuable knowledge, physicians are granted unique social authorities. They are allowed control over medical prescriptions and surgical procedures that others are denied. Given that their understandings enable them to exercise medical powers more effectively than others, they are permitted to make decisions that would land others in jail. A corollary of these strengths is that physicians are uniquely respected.

When they make recommendations, their patients tend to listen. Even when they speak about nonmedical issues, their opinions receive respectful attention.

Furthermore, doctors acquire their special knowledge during an extended and demanding period of socialization. They spend years in medical school and many more in postgraduate training honing an expertise in their specialties. More than this, they are required to learn so much that only demonstrable talent gains a person admission to institutions where the hours of study devoted to difficult materials are nearly beyond human endurance. Yet even after graduation the learning continues. Physicians are expected to participate in a professional culture. They read medical journals, attend medical conferences, and socialize with medical colleagues. In all of these venues, they continue to be judged by colleagues as to their ongoing competence. If they do not measure up, if they do not continue to improve their skills, they may be dismissed as hacks.

The attitudes of one's fellow physicians, however, are more than decorative. Their judgments can be crucial in determining if a doctor will be allowed to practice his or her profession. Doctors belong to self-disciplining associations. They are the ones who are central in deciding if a doctor is guilty of malpractice and should have his or her medical license revoked. Because doctors are the primary custodians of medical knowledge, they are the one's best situated to rule on whether one of their own has strayed. This gives doctors unusual latitude in setting the parameters of how they implement their work.

Last, physicians owe their allegiance to a code of ethics. Before they become full-fledged doctors they must swear to uphold the Hippocratic oath. At minimum, they must promise to do their patients no harm. Physicians who enter a medical career merely to make money are considered unprofessional. Worse still, making a medical decision based on what is most profitable would be regarded as immoral. Doctors are supposed to be the guardians of their patients' welfare. If they do not personally dedicate themselves to this objective, they will be judged to have violated a sacred trust.

All of these characteristics add up to two primary factors. First, as professionals, doctors wield an expertise that others do not. They possess an ability to perform complex tasks where others are inept. Second, doctors are self-motivated to execute their specialties. They do not have to be supervised by bosses in order to ensure that they competently carry out their duties. Together these factors make it possible for society to delegate physicians authority over their own activities. These individuals do not have to be wedged into a bureaucratic structure to force them to do what is required. Thanks to what amounts to a rite of passage, they have become the sort of people who can be relied upon to safeguard the very lives of their patients.

If bureaucracy allows for centralized control, professionalism allows for decentralized control. In lodging special expertise in self-motivated individuals, it makes it possible for these persons to be self-directed. Although they are situated in what amounts to a defined office, they do not require the guidance of a supervisor or of strictly defined rules and procedures to do their jobs. They can be allowed latitude. Indeed, they must be allowed latitude. Without it, they would not be able to apply the expertise that they alone have mastered. Without it, they could not make the spot adjustments to the complicated problems they are called upon to solve.

Professionalism, as opposed to bureaucracy, takes advantage of the virtues of decentralization. It allows professionals to be flexible and responsive in their duties in a way that bureaucratic operatives are denied. They are not forced to follow procedures thought to be most efficient, but can make changes on the spot based on their judgment of what is needed in this particular case. Because they are their own authorities, they can cut through the red tape to individualize their tasks. Thus, if something unexpected comes up, they can adjust to the new circumstances without being constrained by preformulated directives or the commands of distant supervisors.

Consider what it is like to be a psychotherapist. A client comes for help with a personal problem and the two discuss it in the privacy of the therapist's office. As the client's dilemma begins to unfold, the therapist cannot run out of the room to confer with his or her supervisor. He or she must be sufficiently expert to interpret what is occurring then and there. Nor can the therapist consult a rulebook that provides prescriptions for every occasion. He or she must be able to recognize what is different about this case. An inability to do so would reveal a lack of expertise and/or an absence of the personal confidence needed to be helpful to the client. To be missing these qualities is to be unprofessional. More important, it is to deny the client what he or she needs.

This kind of professional independence is more than ever necessary as an increasing number of jobs require special knowledge and self-motivation. Surely lawyers need it. They must be able to think on their feet in the courtroom. Surely financial advisors require it. They must be able to make fiscal plans suitable for a diverse clientele. Even police officers need it. They must be able to apply complex judicial rulings on the street as they interact with an ever more diverse constituency. An evolving techno-commercial society requires extraordinary quantities of complex local knowledge and on-the-spot decision making. As the experience of the Soviet Union demonstrated, a command economy, with everything decided in the middle, is not quick enough on its feet to be efficient.

The McDonaldization thesis tells us that there is a down escalator on which jobs are continuously being deskilled. But there is also an up escalator on which jobs are being professionalized. Many jobs are disappearing as they become automated. But many more require additional years of education. Manufacturing posts are today an increasingly tiny segment of all jobs. Far more people occupy managerial, legal, financial, educational, social service, scientific, engineering, and/or medical positions. It is these individuals who are becoming ever more expert and self-motivated.

BUREAUCRACY VERSUS PROFESSIONALISM

Once most professionals were in private practice. The doctor had his own office in which he was in charge of what he did. The attorney also had his individual practice where he dealt with clients who paid him directly for his services. These professionals were independent in a way that many contemporary professionals envy. Today many of them work within bureaucracies and are salaried just as are other bureaucratic employees. They also have bosses in a way that their predecessors never did. Many of today's physicians work for health maintenance organizations (HMOs). Likewise, many attorneys are employed by industrial corporations.

This emerging circumstance has set up a conflict between professionals and their employers. There now exists a tug-of-war between the centralizing tendencies of bureaucracies and the decentralizing impulses of professionals. Each insists on control of a work product over which both believe they should have authority. Bureaucratic bosses insist that they have the best overview of organizational needs and demand that the professionals under their direction be accountable. The professionals respond that as the experts in what they do, they require the autonomy to make appropriate decisions. Neither side is especially happy with the other and argues that it is best situated to be in charge.

In this contest, the bureaucratic mangers have some advantages. Given that leadership is their business, they can concentrate on providing directions and demanding compliance. They also have the advantage that they are technically in control, at least as defined by the organization. But the professionals also have some high cards. They do possess an expertise that their bosses do not. Although the managers might like to dispense with their services, they cannot. More than they would prefer, they must stand back and allow the professionals to make critical decisions. They are also subject to pressures emanating from professional organizations. In specifying what is ethical, these groups can compel managers to defer to professional standards.

This dispute shows no sign of subsiding anytime soon. Since neither the bureaucrats nor the professionals can do without each other, they are condemned to stare at one another like two scorpions in a bottle. This is a fact of today's organizational life into which new employees are regularly inducted. Peoplization, it seems, is not always a smooth process. Social structures, as well as social norms, are not always conflict free. To become social is also to learn how to cope with the tensions that go with being social. It regularly entails dealing with ambiguities.

Questions

1. What functions does command and control serve in a military organization? What functions does it serve in a commercial organization?

2. Is there an alternative to bureaucracy? Is there another way in which large-scale organizations can be put together?

3. How would you exercise power in a large organization? What strengths or weaknesses would you bring to bear?

4. Do you plan to become a professional? How do you think doing so might change you?

5. Can the disputes between bureaucrats and professionals be resolved? How would you solve them?

Selected Readings

Bellow, A. 2003. *In Praise of Nepotism: A Natural History.* New York: Doubleday.

Blau, P. 1963. *The Dynamics of Bureaucracy.* Chicago: University of Chicago Press.

Grusky, O., and Miller, G. A. (Eds.) 1970. *The Sociology of Organizations: Basic Studies* (2nd ed.). New York: The Free Press.

Larson, M. S. 1977. *The Rise of Professionalism: A Sociological Analysis.* Berkeley: University of California Press.

Simon, H. A. 1947. *Administrative Behavior.* New York: MacMillan.

10

The Numbers Game: Demography and Health

POPULATION

How many siblings do you have? How many siblings did your parents have? What about your grandparents? The chances are that you have one or two. Your parents might have one more. But your grandparents probably came from a much larger family. At the turn of the twentieth century, families with six, eight, or ten children were fairly common. They did not occasion surprise but were thought of sentimentally, that is, as evidence of warm togetherness.

Obviously something changed. But what was it? Why have family-rearing practices so radically transformed? The answer is fairly simple. Blame it on the Industrial Revolution. This technological upheaval not only changed the way people earned a living, but also how they lived their lives. We have already seen how the Industrial Revolution altered the gender division of labor and how it changed the organization of work. But it did more than this. It also changed the size of families, modified interaction between husbands and wives, dramatically increased social mobility, and broke down tribal barriers. As if this weren't enough, it has substantially increased the population of the world, improved personal health, and shifted the places where people live.

Numbers matter. How many people there are in the world can have an enormous impact on a great many things. It can, for starters, make the difference between a *Gemeinschaft* and a *Gesellschaft* world. It can also modify the way people dress, what they eat, and how long they live. It can move them from the farm into the city and set them arguing with each other about whether abortion or euthanasia are moral. Thus, the study of numbers matters. Understanding why and how various populations swell or decline can be crucial to understanding our personal circumstances.

The study of populations is called *demography*. It is about the measurement of peoples. While this may sound dry and uninspiring, it can also be as gripping as arguments over global

115

warming. One of the first practitioners of demography was British clergyman Thomas Malthus. Working about two centuries ago, he became fascinated with population growth. Britain at the time was pioneering the Industrial Revolution and as a result was undergoing a population explosion. Malthus could see that his tight little island was growing more crowded, but he wondered where all this would end. Could an island that had until recently sustained no more than three or four million cope with the arrival of many tens of millions?

Malthus attempted to figure this out intellectually. He sought to project ahead. Population, he realized, multiplies. If two parents have four children, and these children marry and have four children each, and their children do likewise, reasonably soon their progeny will number in the billions. It has been estimated that the entire population of the world during hunter-gatherer times was only about two million. Today the globe is bulging with more than six billion—so Malthus was not that far off. But is this a sustainable figure?

Even two hundred years ago Malthus contemplated how much was too much. He realized that more than raw population data was involved. People had to be fed. So the next question was: How much food would be available? If, reasoned Malthus, a growing population requires additional nutrition, people can respond by planting more acreage. They can add to the land that they cultivate, thereby increasing food production. But the amount of arable land is limited and, moreover, that which is newly farmed will be marginal, hence less productive. Sooner or later one will run up against a ceiling beyond which one cannot go. At this point, there will be a larger number of people than food to feed them.

The way that Malthus framed the problem is that while populations grow geometrically, food supplies increase arithmetically. Given natural rates of human fertility, the former will always outpace the latter. How, then, can populations be kept in check? How can they be prevented from eating themselves out of existence? Malthus believed there were several mechanisms available for achieving a balance. One of these was starvation. Once there was not enough food to sustain them, millions would be wiped out by famine. This was more than an academic conjecture. It has happened many times in the history of the world in places such as India, China, and Africa.

Another mechanism for keeping the population in check was pestilence. Peoples who were weakened by malnutrition would be more susceptible to disease. Horrible plagues would descend on them and again millions would succumb. This too has actually occurred, as with the Black Death in medieval Europe. The third mechanism was war. Peoples who found themselves confronted with hunger would not shrink from invading neighboring territories and appropriating what they needed. In the process of seeking to defeat their foes, they too would cull the population by millions. This has taken place as recently as World War II. One of Hitler's primary purposes in invading the Soviet Union was to seize the Ukrainian breadbasket. Fearful that an expanding German population would soon outgrow its tiny homeland, he enthusiastically contemplated the slaughter of millions of what he considered subhuman Russians. Genghis Kahn's Mongol hordes felt the same way about the Chinese. They massacred over fifty million in order to create more grasslands to pasture their herds.

No doubt, this is an enormously pessimistic stance. Still, Malthus could foresee no other ways out. He and his contemporaries hated these projections, but industrialization seemed to be headed off a demographic cliff. And yet the end has not come. The population has grown, but the predicted genocidal famines and pestilences never entirely arrived. That is because several unforeseen factors intervened. One of these has been the immense improvement in agricultural productivity. Food supplies multiplied when fertilizers, insecticides, labor-saving machinery, and biologically manipulated plants made each acre more fruitful. This made it possible to fill additional bellies, and in places such as the United States, the problem has become an epidemic of obesity rather than starvation.

The other great improvement was in health. One of the offshoots of industrialization was an extension of science, and one of the areas into which science proudly marched was medicine. Where previously a multitude of diseases cut life short, now physicians could make a difference. For the first time in history going to the doctor improved one's chances of survival. For the first time ever, most of the children who were born were likely to survive into old age. Instructive of how radically things had changed was the story of Queen Anne of England. When she died in 1714, she left no surviving heirs. The British were forced to go to Germany to import the Hanoverian king George I. This was not because Anne was barren. To the contrary, she bore well over a dozen children, not one of which survived beyond the age of eleven. Even though she was queen of a major nation, and had access to the best medicine of her day, nothing could be done to save them.

One would have thought that better health would have worsened the Malthusian dilemma, but it did not. As might be expected, it did speed up population growth, but even this spurt was somehow taken in stride. What occurred is this. As nations such as the United States and Britain industrialized, their death rates fell. Improved medicine and improved hygiene meant that fewer children died and that adults lived longer. The birth rate, however, remained constant. In the preindustrial era births and deaths had been more or less balanced. Now births greatly outnumbered deaths. As a consequence, populations soared. More than this, family sizes increased commensurately. Parents continued to have children in accord with cultural standards that evolved to cope with a high infant mortality, with the effect that more of their offspring survived into adulthood.

Eventually parents began to realize that most of their infants would live. They no longer had to produce spares just in case. They also began to recognize that they needed to concentrate greater resources on each child if these youngsters were to be economically successful in an increasingly middle-class world. Specifically, they needed to provide additional schooling if their progeny were to attain professional skills and greater parental attention if they were to acquire habits of self-direction. When this sunk in, family size plummeted. The ideal number of children went down to three and then to two. (In places like China the government went so far as to decree that having more than one child would be illegal.) Within less than a century this culminated in the advanced industrial nations of North America and Europe not even producing sufficient children to replace adults lost through death. Moreover, underdeveloped nations, such as Mexico, seemed to be following the same sequence. As their economies improved, their populations and family sizes grew. Yet as they became more prosperous, their fertility rates declined as well. Malthusian predictions of doom could apparently be held in check by voluntary efforts to limit family size. Malthus himself did not believe this was possible, yet experience demonstrated that it was.

HEALTH AND HYGIENE

Improved health has been a primary engine in population growth, but how did these advances come about? What changed so that fewer people died of disease or other biological causes?

Before attempting to solve this mystery, however, here is a puzzling question. Which occupation is responsible for saving more lives than any other? As you will probably guess, the answer is not *physicians.* That would be too obvious. *Nurses* is not the correct response either. Nor is *pharmacists.* Not even the *police* or members of the *military* are responsible for the quantum leaps in personal survival. Have you figured it out yet? The surprising answer is *garbage collectors.* They have been the most steadfast protectors of our well-being.

How, it will be asked, can this be? What does picking up trash have to do with saving lives? The reason this seems a strange conjunction is that modern Americans are spoiled. We are so accustomed to having heaps of garbage whisked away that we cannot imagine what it was like when people threw their refuse out the window. We forget, if we ever knew, that men are supposed to walk on the street side when they accompany a woman because this is where the household wastes would land. Nor do we understand why people say it is raining cats and dogs when there is a heavy downpour. Since we do not live in a world where dead animals are swept through the streets on these occasions, their rotting carcasses never come to mind. Nor do we live in world, like that of the American colonies, where the authorities purchased municipal pigs to roam through the city lanes so as to consume edible trash. We are even spared the mountains of manure that streets overflowing with horses once produced.

In the days when trash was everywhere people could believe that flies were spontaneously generated in piles of refuse. But they did not realize that these heaps of waste were really breeding grounds for disease. Totally unaware of the role germs play in producing illness, they saw no need to inhibit the procreation of invisible agents of death. It surely never occurred to them that infectious agents transmitted from rats and fleas to people had caused the Black Death. The consequence of this ignorance was that they saw no point in picking up the garbage; hence epidemics spread like wildfire, especially in urban areas.

Contaminated water was also a problem. In places like London, right through the nineteenth century, cholera was a scourge. Every few years it killed several thousands of people. But no one knew how to stop it. The best that could be done was for the rich to escape to their country estates. The poor, of course, were left behind to perish. This is where science stepped in. A habit of investigating natural phenomena prompted the investigation of this one too. Why, men of science wanted to know, were so many people dying? And why were they dying in the city and not the country?

Epidemiology was then in its infancy, but one of the things that could be done was to map out the areas of the greatest die-offs. It very quickly became evident that the highest mortality clustered around municipal water spigots. When this information was combined with the germ theory, what was occurring could be deciphered. As was known from first-hand experience, cholera is an intestinal disease. Its primary symptom is extreme diarrhea. Victims evacuate so much tainted material from their bowels that they become dehydrated, and it is this dehydration that eventually kills them. What the investigators realized was that in a city where going to the bathroom still meant using an outhouse, the germ-infected discharges that the ill transferred into these was leaching down through the soil into the nearby Thames River. From here it was being pumped back uphill to the very spigots from which most of the inhabitants obtained their drinking water. Thus was created a cycle of disease and death.

Once this was understood, prophylactic measures became possible. The city fathers first built a pipe to conduct uncontaminated water from upriver into the city wells. Then they constructed a sewer system to conduct waste downriver where it could safely be released back into the Thames. With this accomplished, cholera was tamed. People could now live and work within the city limits without fear of periodically being cut down by an invisible executioner.

What also helped to improve sanitation the invention of the flush toilet. In the days of Henry VIII, the floors of his palaces were covered not in carpets, but in reeds. This was because his courtiers might relieve themselves when and wherever their internal plumbing prompted them. They also threw pieces of unfinished food on the flooring as well. The reeds made this muck simpler to clean up. Water closets came later. Thanks to nineteenth-century entrepreneurs such as Thomas Crapper, indoor facilities came into vogue. These could now be connected to the newly constructed sewer system, making it even more effective. Eventually the plumbing system became so sophisticated that sufficient water was available for people to take regular baths. Earlier bathwater was a luxury. People would soak in a tub maybe once or twice a year. So pungent did they become that during the Middle Ages perfume became a vital adjunct of social life.

Only by the twentieth century did people begin to worry about things like pure food and drugs. Only then were regulations enacted to ensure that manufacturers and food processors took care with the materials they sold to the public. Novels such as *The Jungle* alerted the public to the unhygienic conditions prevailing in the meat-packing industry. So scandalized were they at learning that rat feces and human digits were routinely incorporated in their sausages that they demanded federal regulation. They also demanded controls over the drugs that were sold over the counter. No longer could Coca Cola be laced with cocaine. No longer would patent medicines be big business, with Grandma sipping a medication that converted her into an addict.

All in all, with progress in industrialization came a myriad of healthful measures that reduced public exposure to disease-producing agents. People began to say that cleanliness was next to godliness. They also began to demand that foods be individually packaged rather than having to dip into a communal pickle barrel. They were especially pleased when modest inventions, such as cellophane, made it possible to protect the freshness and purity of their purchases. What is more, they actually took to taking daily showers. To do less began to seem disgusting.

HEALTH AND MEDICINE

Most of us do not realize just how primitive medical treatment was until very recently. Perhaps we know that the prevailing dogma in Western medicine before the germ theory was that of the four humors. These four fluids, each of which corresponded to one of the four elements of which the world was thought to be composed, supposedly controlled the body. Equivalent to earth, air, fire, and water were blood, phlegm, black bile, and yellow bile. Physicians held that if these fluids were in balance, then a person would be healthy, but if not, then the person would not be healthy. Blood was particularly significant because it could be more easily regulated than the other humors. Thus, if a doctor decreed there was too much of this substance, bleeding a patient could reduce its volume.

Today we may imagine that leaches were used to accomplish this feat, but these were a late addition. Most of the time a lancet, that is, a small knife, was used to cut into a vein. So common was this practice that medieval hospitals featured troughs to carry the excess blood outside. So widespread was the practice that when George Washington came down with a bad cold after an inspection tour of Mount Vernon, this was the treatment prescribed by his doctor. And when he did not immediately respond by getting well, he was bled again and again until he expired. In this, he was not alone. Many millions of others were ushered out of life by such medical remedies. Samuel Pepys knew this. In his famous seventeenth-century diary he opined that he would rather suffer the agony of urinary stones than undergo an operation he was certain would result in his demise.

Before the Industrial Revolution, to say that anatomical knowledge was primitive would be an understatement. The Greeks, for instance, believed that the heart was a furnace, not a pump. Not until the research of Harvey in the early 1600s was it even realized that blood circulates around the body. Nevertheless, an account of the standard views concerning a condition until recently identified as hysteria is especially instructive. The Greeks named this disorder after the female womb, which in their language is called the *hystera*—ergo the term *hysterectomy*. This behavioral pattern, which is characterized by excessive emotionality, was thought to be confined to women because it was believed to be caused when the uterus broke loose from its normal moorings and began to travel around the body. Regarded almost like an independent little animal, the preferred cures were contingent on inducing the uterus to return to its proper location. This might be accomplished in one of two ways. The first remedy advised that honey be rubbed on the woman's vulva so as to attract the womb back down. The other stipulated that smelling salts be placed under her nose so as to frighten it into descending.

It was not until after the Renaissance when the Catholic Church again allowed anatomical dissections that is was realized the uterus was not free to move about. But this did not end the biological errors. Since physicians remained convinced that the uterus caused a woman's symptoms, they devised a reworked theory to explain them. Now it was hypothesized that a patient's light-headedness was attributable to gases floating up from her womb. These gases were referred to as vapors; hence a hysterical woman was said to be suffering from a case of the vapors and smelling salts might still be prescribed to snap her back into sanity. This account, of course, was also totally mistaken. Today we understand that men too can suffer from histrionic personality disorders, which most psychiatrists now attribute to faulty socialization.

Mental conditions, in general, were badly misunderstood. They were habitually regarded as evidence demonic possession, in which case they might be treated by exorcism. Even when these states were regarded as being of biological origin, patients were normally punished as if they were moral lepers. They might be locked up in dungeons, blistered with caustic agents, or medicated with emetics that turned their stomachs inside out. Even so prominent a patient as king George III of England was not exempt. When he came down with an illness in retrospect diagnosed as porphyria, he was strapped to a chair and occasionally scourged with whips.

Another egregious sort of medical error, albeit one with more lethal consequences, concerns septicemia. Some years ago a sociologist friend decided to carry out a demographic study of his own family. In so doing, he discovered that its roots were prerevolutionary and that many of his ancestors were quite prosperous. But he also uncovered something more startling. When he looked into the mortality rates of his precursors, he found that the life expectancy of both the men and the women increased right up to the Civil War era. That is when he encountered an unexpected spike in female mortality rates. The reason, he learned, was related to their affluence. Because they had money and were well educated, they were more inclined than their neighbors to seek medical aid in times of need. This included childbirth. In a period when most women still depended upon midwives to assist in delivering their infants, his relatives utilized hospitals and physicians for this purpose.

Ironically, in their efforts to be progressive, these people placed their women in jeopardy. The midwives washed their hands before entering a woman's bed chamber, but doctors did not believe in implementing an "old wives" tale. In their hospitals, they went from sawing a man's leg off in one room to assisting in childbirth in another without ever cleaning the blood off their hands. As a consequence, they routinely transferred infectious agents from one patient to another. In so doing, they induced many fatal diseases. Women did not succumb to pregnancy per se, but to an iatrogenically produced illness when exposed to germs never encountered at home. It was not until antiseptic measures were introduced at the end of the nineteenth century that is blight subsided.

This was also about the time that anesthetics were introduced. Before this, limbs were cut off without the benefit of any better painkiller than alcohol. Surgeons were then regarded as little better than butchers, with their skill measured in the speed with which they could hack through bone. So fast were some of these poorly trained doctors that it was not unusual for them to saw off one of their own fingers in the process.

It was really the twentieth century that saw the burgeoning of modern medicine. It was only then that wonder drugs were discovered. Antibiotics have become customary fare, but before they arrived millions yielded their lives to contagious diseases today perceived as trivial. We think of measles as a childhood rite of passage, yet there was a time when so many died from it that Athens nearly lost its war with Sparta on account of this illness. We likewise take modern surgical operations in stride. We no longer expect to perish from these procedures, but anticipate that even one as delicate as open-heart surgery will be successful. If it is not, we are scandalized. On such occasions we may even contemplate suing the surgeon for malpractice.

Today we take heroic medical treatments for granted. We expect that anytime we get sick our doctors will be able to figure out what is wrong and find a way to cure us. Even when we enter old age, we expect to be prescribed the appropriate pill and/or referred for the suitable medical procedure. These efforts may be contingent on enormously expensive technology, but, when it comes to our health, cost is deemed of little consequence. This, in turn, has placed a burden on medical insurance, whether administered by the government or private companies. People now expect so much that we, as a nation, may have bumped up against the limits of our resources.

There is also the problem that heroic interventions can simply prolong a person's suffering. An elderly patient whose bodily functions are in the process of shutting down may nevertheless be kept alive by tubes connected to virtually every orifice. Individuals and their families are thus confronted with a question their ancestors never faced. They must decide whether to enjoin medical personnel to refrain from resuscitating them should they undergo a physiological crisis while in a medical facility. Indeed, some have taken to writing "living wills" to instruct their doctors what they should do if their physical condition precludes them from providing instructions more directly during the emergency. How significant these issues have become has recently been highlighted by several celebrated cases of patients in vegetative states. If someone has been so severely injured in an automobile accident that doctors describe the victim as brain dead, should the patient be kept alive by artificial means? Opinions are passionately divided on this question. Some say respect for life must triumph over every other consideration, while others shudder that the thought of being kept alive while not animated in any ordinary sense.

This dilemma has also surfaced with respect to euthanasia. Medicine has become so competent at prolonging life that many people—among them the extremely elderly and the painfully ill—have claimed the right to kill themselves rather than endure ongoing agonies. Some have also sought legalized assistance from medial personnel. Dr. Kevorkian famously championed this option. Yet the jury remains out as to whether society as a whole will tolerate, let alone recommend, this sort of intervention.

Another therapeutic conundrum has arisen with respect to abortion. During epochs when most children perished shortly after birth, questions about terminating pregnancies rarely came up. It made little sense to kill a fetus when one could not be certain that any of one's progeny would survive. The advent of modern medicine accompanied by a middle-class mentality changed all of this. Unwanted pregnancies could now safely be ended even late in a woman's term. It is this development that sparked the current controversy between pro-life and pro-choice contingents. Radicals on one side currently demand that abortions be abolished no matter what, whereas radicals on the other, with equal fervor, insist that it be allowed under almost any circumstance. Society has not yet reached a consensus on this question either, but it would never have come up had not medicine so dramatically reduced the occurrence of infant mortality.

THE GERONTOLOGICAL REVOLUTION

If people are not dying as frequently, then more of them must be getting older. This is not just a logical conclusion, but an absolute fact. It is not too strong to state that we are undergoing a gerontological revolution. The numbers of persons living into old age has grown so rapidly as to constitute a sea change in the way society is organized. Where once, with respect to age, societies look like pyramids, today they look more like rectangles. Throughout most of history, the overwhelming majority of those residing within human communities were young. The median age would have been in the late teens or early twenties. Life expectancy itself was such that few survived beyond the mid-century point. As a result, social institutions were arranged to deal with an age distribution skewed toward the low side.

But now that modern medicine is keeping people alive longer, and now that parents are also having fewer offspring, the age distribution has been profoundly altered. Thus, when Social Security was introduced into the United States, the retirement age was set at sixty-five because few people survived beyond this point. Today a very large segment of the population does. Many now even survive past the century mark. During the time of Henry VIII, when he got into his late forties, he was considered an old man. And when he died of a leg abscess in his early fifties, few thought that he had expired prematurely. Today such a death would be viewed as tragic.

Nowadays the overwhelming numbers of people in advanced societies are adults. As a result, the kinds of services they require and the opportunities available to them have been profoundly transformed. A society with fewer children and more seniors needs fewer nursery schools but more nursing homes. Likewise, if there are a greater number of people making it into their fifties and sixties, there will be fewer openings in the upper echelons of the executive suite for ambitious twenty-somethings. By the same token, the types of jobs available will be altered. There will clearly be more positions in the medical field, but fewer as elementary school teachers.

Among the resultant problems are the impending crises in Social Security and Medicare. Back in the 1930s, when Franklin Roosevelt overhauled Social Security, the ratio of retirees to those contributing into the retirement system was more than fifteen to one. In other words, for every person collecting a Social Security check, over fifteen were paying into the system. This has so significantly changed that we are approaching a circumstance where there will be only two paying for each one collecting. And since those who are collecting live longer, they will be receiving more than they contribute. A little elementary math should make it plain that such a system must eventually become insolvent. Unless there is reform—and right now there is little public appetite either for raising personal contributions or for deferring the age of retirement— bankruptcy is inevitable.

A similar financial emergency looms in Medicare. If more and more people require a host of more expensive medical interventions, the dollars available to do the job inexorably grow less adequate. There will surely come a time when taxes will have to be raised to confiscatory levels if recipients are to receive the services for chronic conditions that they demand. Of course, this cannot happen. People cannot be taxed more than they earn. A level of pain will eventually be reached where the public will decide to cap what is provided—either that or the entire system will have to be revised such that people pay only for the benefits they receive, which would provide an incentive for them to cut back on services no longer perceived as free.

Less frequently considered a consequence of the gerontological revolution, but of equally great importance, is the issue of retirement. When Social Security first came on the scene, retirement was eagerly sought. People expected to reach a date when they would not have to work, but could engage in recreational activities instead. Most people understood that this period of retirement would be relatively short, yet they hoped that their health would be sufficient to take advantage of their freedom. They mused about going fishing, golfing, or taking a trip around the world. Few imagined that they would grow weary of an existence released from vocational demands.

What had not been contemplated was that retirement might last two, three, and sometimes four decades. A person taking an early retirement at sixty-two, yet living into his nineties, would have to do a lot of fishing, golfing, or traveling to fill thirty-some unstructured years. While working on an assembly line unbounded leisure might sound enticing, but the reality could be excruciatingly dull. Nor would the diminution of status that typically goes with retirement be appreciated. Working on a job, especially one that entails responsibility, furnishes a person with respect. One is understood to be contributing to the community and holding down a position of substance. A retiree is, however, a supernumerary. He or she has become superfluous. Such a person can safely be disregarded. This outcome often motivates people to continue working even after they could retire. Yet what will they do if more of them make this choice? The way careers are presently organized, people are expected to step down at a certain age. But if they do, what kinds of work will they substitute for their previous employments? And will these constitute a second career? Will these second careers require additional training? This is one more area in which social norms are evolving.

And what about the women? If they are having fewer children, and also living longer, then the proportion of their lives devoted to child rearing must perforce decline. So what will they do when their youngsters leave the nest? We are already seeing the outlines of an answer. Many more are returning to school so that they can acquire the credentials for stimulating employments outside the home. They are concurrently moving up within commercial and governmental organizations as well. Apparently once freed from their parental responsibilities, they are at liberty to direct their energies to other interests. In so doing, they have become more successful in ventures not previously associated with their gender and they now constitute a larger segment of even managerial ranks. How will the workplace respond to their emergent power? Will this further modify the gender division of labor? We shall see.

URBANISM AND SUBURBANISM

When the twentieth century was new, people fondly sang about marrying the girl next door. City living was a relatively new phenomenon and having potential mates so close at hand was an exciting prospect. For most of history, the largest part of humanity has lived out on the farm, or perhaps in a village close by their fields. Neighbors were thus few and far between. Urbanism was, as a consequence, quite a change. A product of both industrialization and rising population densities, city living enabled people to settle near the factories where they worked. But this also made it possible to live in close proximity to a variety of social amenities. Things that as isolated peasants they could never imagine were now easily available.

One of the changes was in transportation. The steam engine had first powered manufacturing plants, but it was soon adapted to ships and railroads. In town, tracked vehicles first became streetcars and then subway systems. This permitted people to move quickly from one end of a municipality to another. As such, their shopping was no longer confined to their immediate vicinity. They could now go downtown to make purchases at the newly invented department stores. Where once products were fabricated and sold in the same small quarters, an array of factories began to ship their output to large-scale establishments that were accessible to thousands of customers. This enabled these emporiums to carry a wide variety of products. Ordinary people now had choices never before available.

There were also options in cultural activities. Prior to the industrial era, what is now called classical music was sponsored by aristocrats for aristocrats. The chambers in which what we call chamber music was played were within the precincts of their palaces. Theaters in which more romantic fare was made available to the masses could not exist without a plethora of paying customers who could reach them by public transportation. Similar considerations apply to art. Paintings were once exclusively for the delectation of the nobility, but urbanization made it feasible to construct museums open to the larger community. Even fancy restaurants were a benefit of the demographic impact of industrialization. In this case, swanky chefs whose only clientele had been members of the gentry could begin to earn a living by catering to a broader constituency.

There were also new entertainments such as amusement parks. Places like New York City's Coney Island burst into prominence. Electric trains permitted masses of common laborers to patronize wonders such as the roller coaster at Dreamland or to bathe at beaches where millions of them came to escape the heat of summer. They could also travel to racetracks and baseball stadiums to enjoy spectator sports as they never could in years past. Urban life was thus filled with distractions that feudal peasants had not so much as contemplated.

Compared to this the suburbs of the late twentieth century have been condemned as barren sprawl. They have been execrated as lonely wastelands where middle-class conformists suffer in isolation in their standalone houses surrounded by neatly manicured lawns. They are said not to know their neighbors, never mind to celebrate the prospect of marrying the girl next door. Instead, miles and miles of uniform mediocrity encircle them. Demanding that forest and meadow alike be paved over, they heedlessly destroy the environment upon which we are all dependent.

Yet this is a caricature. Derived from observations of the external standardization of early suburban developments such as Levittown, these descriptions mischaracterize what is occurring as people move out of urban centers to the metropolitan periphery. The middle classes, that is, the folks who invented the suburbs, are not robotic conformists. To the contrary, they are self-directed strivers. As their numbers have increased, they have sought the comfort and safety of the suburbs. In search of conclaves where they can better educate their young and in which more opportunities are available, they have largely been successful in this quest.

Unlike the urban pioneers of yore, they are not dependent upon public transportation, but on the private automobile. More prosperous than their forebears, they can afford houses with two- and three-car garages—and the automobiles, powerboats, and off-road vehicles with which to fill them. If they do not dream of marrying the girl next door—and they don't—it is because they have the mobility to seek mates farther afield. When they go courting, they may venture many dozens of miles from their homes; hence they do not have to inquire about whether a potential date lives nearby.

Contrary to what the critics claim, the suburbs are even more about choice than the central cities of old. Perhaps the best place to begin a search for this diversity is by touring one of the local supermarkets. (Local in this case means within automobile rage.) These markets have grown monstrously large. They have burgeoned into huge bazaars offering a cornucopia of sundries. A journey down a single one of their dozens of aisles reveals scores of cereal brands from which to choose. The problem now is not finding a product that will meet one's needs, but of selecting between a plethora of goods that might.

The larger number of potential customers has also spawned the suburban mall. Here many dozens of merchandisers sell everything from clothing and sporting goods to beauty products and furniture. Department stores and discount houses now congregate together in commercial zones ringed by acres of free parking. Some malls even have their own amusement parks. Almost all boast food courts in which shoppers can indulge their tastes for pizza, hot dogs, or Japanese fast food. Should they venture outside the mall, suburbanites will find a wealth of more exotic restaurants. Everything from Chinese buffets to phony Polynesian eateries to Mexican restaurants and Italian bistros beckon the would-be epicure. It seems that each new ethnic group that makes its way to America eventually sets up a culinary outpost in the hinterlands, the Thai and the Ethiopians not excluded.

Nor are the suburbs bereft of the cultural amenities of the urban center. They too boast a surplus of sporting choices. Everything from golf courses to tennis courts to swimming pools and little league baseball games are in easy reach. So too is high culture. Many suburbs have their own symphony orchestras and/or community theaters. They also boast a plethora of movie houses, libraries, and colleges. What is more, thanks to the automobile, interstate highways, and the remnants of mass transit, suburbanites have access to urban amenities as well. They can travel downtown to witness professional sports, to attend the opera and ballet, to peruse the museums, or to go to public lectures. They do not have to be isolated if they do not wish to be.

Finally, suburbanites, like urbanites, today live within a more diverse world than did their ancestors. Unparalleled prosperity and advances in transportation have launched folk migrations of unprecedented magnitude. Peoples from every corner of the world can travel to almost any other corner of the world. Some destinations, of course, are more favored than others. One of these has been America, and this includes the suburbs as well as the cities. Citizens of the United States, almost wherever they live, can rub shoulders with people raised in different cultures. Even if they do not travel far themselves—although most do—they can expand their consciousness by picking the brains of others who think differently from themselves. This too is a consequence of recent industrially inspired demographic transformations.

Questions

1. What do you believe is the ideal size for a family? Why do you believe this?
2. Are there too many people in the world? What is your solution for overpopulation?
3. How should public health care be financed? What about Medicare and Social Security?
4. Do you believe that abortion should be legal? Should there be any limits on it? What about euthanasia?
5. Has suburbanism become a social problem? Should it be condemned as sprawl? Where would you prefer to live? Why?

Selected Readings

Balaker, T., and Staley, S. 2006. *The Road More Traveled: Why the Congestion Crisis Matters More Than You Think.* Lanham: Rowman and Littlefield Publishers.

Cumston, C. C. 1987. *The History of Medicine: From the Time of the Pharaohs to the End of the XVIII Century.* New York: Dorset Press.

Fishman, R. 1987. *Bourgeois Utopias: The Rise and Fall of Suburbia.* New York: Basic Books.

Gans, H. J. 1967. *The Levittowners: Way of Life and Politics in a New Suburban Community.* New York: Alfred A. Knopf.

Jackson, K. T. 1985. *Crabgrass Frontier: The Suburbanization of the United States.* New York: Oxford University Press.

Satel, S. 2000. *PC, M.D.: How Political Correctness Is Corrupting Medicine.* New York: Basic Books.

Addendum

Research Methods
Miriam W. Boeri

How do we know what we know? For example, how do you know that if you put your hand in fire, it will be burned? Well, most of you tried this a few times when you were younger, or maybe at parties with friends. The point is you learned by experience. You put you finger in a flame, or touched the stove burner, and it hurt. But what about other things we know? How do you know that the chair you are sitting on will hold you? How do you know that cars will stop at a red light so you can cross the street? How do you know that if you work really hard on your class paper you will get a good grade? For many of these questions we rely on what usually works. We do not really know if the chair will hold us, or if the car will stop at the red light, but past experience informs us that it usually does. Therefore we assume it will be the same in most cases, and we live our lives on assumptions. But do you always get a good grade if you work really hard? Sometimes you may have felt that you worked hard, and yet you still got a bad grade. Maybe you were upset at the professor. Perhaps you complained and said, "but I worked really hard on this." Perhaps the professor responded with something like "it wasn't good enough," or "you did not do what I wanted you to do." Most of the assumptions work for us, but sometimes they do not. You do not always get a good grade if you work hard. Sometimes there are certain facts about getting a good grade that you need to find out.

There are usually two main ways that you know what you know: (1) something worked for you in the past, and (2) you heard or read it from another source.

Let's look a little more into the first way of knowing things. If something worked for you in the past, you assume it will work again. The more it works for you the greater your belief that this is indeed a fact. That might hold true for sitting on a chair, but not for everything. To find out what the professor wants on your paper, you may have to read the instructions on the syllabus. If this does not provide enough information, you might ask other students in the class who did get good grades on the paper. Consider other ways you "conduct research" to get answers to your questions.

What I am trying to show you is that we all conduct research in our daily lives. When the questions are important enough, we do some research. For example, finding the best pizza in town, choosing where you will rent or buy a house, and deciding on a career are decisions that require research. For questions that do not concern us too personally, we usually accept what we hear or are told. Unfortunately, we accept many so-called facts that are merely myths and are not based on well-supported facts. You may have heard the statement that "old people are unsafe drivers." We notice that when someone is driving below speed limit, causing other drivers to engage in dangerous passing maneuvers, it always seems to be an older driver. Or is it just that we notice or remember when it is an older driver because it fits with our preconceived assumption? If we look at rates found in police reports, we find that younger drivers are more likely to cause accidents than are older drivers. So what is the fact? Who is the unsafe driver?

By now some of you might be asking the question: "What do you mean by unsafe driver?" That is a great question, because if we do not establish what an unsafe driver means—if we do not agree on what it means—we cannot find an answer to the question. If we define unsafe as causing accidents, the answer appears to be that young adults are more unsafe.

Learning how research is conducted will help you find answers to your own questions as well as assess whether the facts you read, hear, or see are founded on good research. The discipline of sociology is based on answers found through research to social questions. Some questions require years of research and some of the findings are still being debated. (Some of these debates were discussed in Chapter 2.) Some social questions are important for all or for society, such as "What causes people to commit crime?" Other questions may be important only to certain groups of people, such as "Why do people get tattoos?" In the field of sociology we use the scientific method to answer these questions.

Research methods provide a systematic plan for finding answers. The basic steps in the research process are as follows:

1. *Define the topic of investigation:* What is the topic you are interested in studying or learning more about?

2. *Conduct a literature review:* Find out what others have learned about the topic. Usually this is facilitated by a literature search on the topic in the library or through online sources, such as academic journal articles.

3. *Assess the requirements for carrying out the research:* How much money, time, and access to resources do you have to conduct this research? For example, it would be difficult for you to conduct research on what presidents of universities think about grade inflation since you do not have easy access to college presidents other than perhaps the president of your own college. However, you can conduct research on what students think of grade inflation because you have ready access to students.

4. *Specify the research questions:* Once you have a topic in mind and have carefully read what has already been written about this topic and all sides of the argument, you should write a specific research question covering what you want to find out in your research study. Suppose you are interested in cheating on exams. The research question can be descriptive (How do students cheat on exams?), or it can look for a causal relationship (Why do students cheat on exams?). Sometimes research explores areas where little is known (What is going on in a student's head as he or she is cheating?).

5. *Consider the ethical issues:* What is the motive behind doing this research? If you are conducting research on people, are you allowing them to consent to being studied? Does the research hurt anyone? What do the findings add to our knowledge? Today, we have review boards that review proposed research in order to point out any ethical areas to consider that researchers might not be aware of due to their personal involvement in the research. Review boards protect those being studied, and protect the researcher from making any unintended mistakes.

6. *Devise a research strategy (design):* There are two basic ways to conduct research:

    (1) Quantitative research methods: Typically, quantitative methods use empirical data that can be converted into numbers.

    (2) Qualitative research methods: Qualitative methods use various forms of data, but typically they are presented in words.

7. *Gather the data:* Data are pieces of information. In sociology you use what is called "empirical" data, which means the data can be proven by one of your sense. You can see, feel, touch, smell, or hear those pieces of information. Once you decide on the research question and strategy, you need to choose whom you will gather data from and how many individuals will be included in your sample. For example, will you interview students, conduct surveys with people in the mall, or observe fans at a baseball game? More strategies used in the research design are described later in this section.

8. *Interpret or analyze the data:* Quantitative data is analyzed using statistical methods. Most researchers use a statistical program, such as SPSS, to do this analysis, but they first need to know what they are doing. This requires some knowledge of statistics. Qualitative data is analyzed in many different ways. Typically, researchers analyze qualitative data to look for patterns or categories and then explain how and why they are interpreting the data as they do. Whereas quantitative analysis describes the data using numbers, qualitative analysis describes the data using words.

9. *State your conclusions:* What did you find out? How were your research questions answered? Simply describing what you found is not enough. You need to also explain what this means, and more specifically how it answers your original research questions.

10. *Share your results:* Present or publish your research in some form.

RESEARCH DESIGNS OR STRATEGIES

The heart of the research study is step 6—the strategy you will use, and step 7—how you will gather the data. This deserves more explanation because there are different strategies in both quantitative and qualitative research designs. As you will see, which design you choose depends on your research questions. Since a content analysis design can be used in both quantitative and qualitative research methods, we must explain the differences between these basic strategies. Content analysis can be used as a quantitative or a qualitative method design. Content analysis involves analyzing the content of something (e.g., books, movies, websites, etc). In a quantitative method format, you will convert the content to numerical measurements. In a qualitative format you will use words to analyze the content. For example, if your research question is "Are older women underrepresented in magazine ads?" you need to use a *quantitative method*. After selecting a sample of magazines, you count all the women in the magazine ads. Next you decide how you will identify if a woman is older (e.g., grey hair, wrinkles, etc). You then count the older women and calculate the percentage of all women in the magazine who are older. Next you compare the percentage of older women in the magazine to the percentage of older women in society to answer your question about whether or not they are underrepresented. Questions and answers in quantitative designs are very specific.

If your research question is "How are older women represented in magazine ads?" you need to use a *qualitative method*. Again, collect your magazines and decide how you will identify who is an older woman. Then describe all the ads of older women in words. Is there a pattern of how they are represented? Does it fit reality? Many questions can be answered using a qualitative method, and this design allows you more freedom in how you will interpret your answers.

Experiments are a type of quantitative method because they produce data that are numerical. Experiments include many different strategies. We will cover only one type here as an example. If your research question is "Do movies help students learn the material?" you can use an experimental design. A professor might teach two classes exactly the same way, except one will include movies and the other will not. At the end of the semester she compares the class grades (converted to numbers). If the class that included movies received better grades on average, then movies help the students learn the material. Of course this design makes some very big assumptions, and we do not know whether these are correct or not. For example, do the students in each class compare in skills and learning ability? Is the professor measuring learning in the way the grades are assessed? Sociological experiments are difficult to conduct on people and often raise ethical issues. For example, if the professor discovers halfway through the class by the midterm grades that students that have the movies do much better, should the experiment be stopped and movies be included in both classes? (As mentioned in Chapter 2, experiments are not often conducted in sociological research studies.)

Surveys are standard strategy of collecting data, particularly in social science research. Surveys typically include questions that can be answered with numbers or answers that are converted to numbers. Since they collect numerical data, surveys are often used in quantitative research methods. Surveys can be collected by asking respondents to complete the survey with paper and pencil (self-administered), by the researcher asking the respondent the questions and writing the answers (face-to-face meeting), over the phone, or by computer. A current method of collecting surveys is computer-assisted telephone interviews (CATI), in which a researcher calls the respondent on the phone and completes the survey on the computer. Whatever method is used, the responses will be computed and analyzed using statistical methods. This means the data will be described with numbers—for example, the percentage of males and females who agree that you should not kiss on a first date, or whether the difference reported by males and females on this question is significant.

Observation designs are often a qualitative method since the data are typically presented in words. The research questions are usually concerned with interactions between people that can be observed. Observations must be nonobtrusive—the researchers must not interfere with what they are observing in any way. The researcher becomes an objective tool and tries to eliminate any preconceived bias in his or her interpretation of what is going on. For example, suppose your research question is "How do men pick up women at a bar?" You would then spend hours at the bar observing men picking up women. Typically, you would write your notes as soon as you get home or to the car. You would repeat this every night for hours until you have enough data to see a pattern. Nonobtrusive observation should only be conducted in public areas. Conducting such research in a private setting without the participants' consent is considered unethical.

Another type of observation research is *participant observation.* In this case the researcher becomes part of the group under research as a participant. Typically, the group members know the researcher is conducting research on them. This is referred to as *overt participant observation.* Conducting *covert* participant observation would be considered unethical. Participant observers usually do not become complete participants but instead spend hours with the people under study. Also, the research question is usually exploratory. For example, if you want to know what homeless people do all day, one way to do this is to join the homeless on the street, explain that you are a researcher, and follow them through the day. You would not necessarily need to sleep where they are sleeping. Spending days with a group of people you are unfamiliar with provides rich details if you are good at taking notes and recording your observations. Some forms of participant observation are called *ethnography.* This type of participant observation involves weeks and sometimes years of participating with your research subjects in their own location (also known as *field research*).

Most researchers do not have the time to spend weeks in the field. Another type of qualitative method often used is the *in-depth interview.* Interviews are typically conducted face to face and are tape-recorded. In contrast to the type of questions asked in surveys, which have predetermined answers (closed-ended), questions asked in this type of interview allow the respondent to expand or diverge into other areas. For example, instead of asking "Do you agree with legalizing drugs?" which can be answered with a simple yes or no, an in-depth interviewer would ask "What do you think about the legalization of drugs?" The in-depth interview allows the respondent to express more than a yes-or-no answer. For example, the respondent might discuss legality in certain cases, or for certain drugs, or with certain restrictions. In-depth interviews are very complex to analyze. A yes-or-no response can be reported as: "60 percent of the participants responded that drugs should not be legalized" or "35 percent of the males thought drugs should not be legalized, while 50 percent of females thought they should not be legalized." The findings of the in-depth interview responses might be organized by themes, categories, or types. For example, "four types of responses were found: (1) those who think all drugs should be legalized, (2) those who felt only some drugs should be legalized, (3) those who felt that some drugs should be dispensed as medication by doctors, (4) and those who felt that no drugs should be legalized." Each type of response would then be illustrated with some quotes from the interviews.

Like content analysis, *secondary data analysis* can be used in a quantitative or qualitative method. Secondary data analysis means the researcher will analyze data that has already been collected. Typically, the data is in numerical form and has been collected by government agencies, such as police reports or U.S. Census data. For example, if a researcher wants to know if earlier closing of bars and establishments that sell alcohol has an effect on DUI arrests, the researcher can examine public records on DUI arrests in areas where bars are required to close earlier and compare that data with arrest data from areas where bars close later.

Questions

1. Discuss a topic of research with another student. Follow the research steps together and develop a research question and design.
2. Locate a journal article on a research topic of interest. Be sure to find an article that has a methods section, or it is not a research paper but another type of paper, such as a thesis. Read the article and identify all the parts of the research design.

Selected Readings

Babbie, Earl R. 2006. *The Basics of Social Research.* Belmont, CA: Thomson Wadsworth.

Neuman, W. Lawrence. 2006. *The Basics of Social Research: Qualitative and Quantitative Approaches.* Boston, MA: Allyn & Bacon, Inc.

Pyrczak, Fred, and Bruce, Randall R. 1999. *Writing Empirical Research Reports.* Glendale, CA: Pyrczak Publishing.